# Foreword

I have very much pleasure in writing this Foreword for this book by Dr. Edgar Jones.

It is a much needed book. For some reason Old Testament scholars have not been consumed with the same desire to communicate as New Testament scholars have been; and the material suitable for the inquiring laymen is less plentiful on the Old Testament than it is on the New Testament.

Dr. Jones has written an excellent book from two points of view. In the first place he deals with great subjects and to deal with great subjects is a great step on the way to writing a great book. And secondly, although he is a scholar of the first order he nevertheless writes with a simplicity, a lucidity, and with the verve which makes his book universally readable. I have no doubt at all that this book will be of great use to the Preacher, to the Teacher, to the Student and to the inquiring person who wishes to find out more about his Bible.

This is an excellent book, an informative book, and a book which any interested person can read and profit by.

**William Barclay**

# God, Man
# and Community

## More Old Testament Words

## by
## Edgar Jones

John Paul  The Preacher's Press

God, Man and Community
first published in Great Britain
1974

by John Paul the Preacher's Press
Charlton House, Hunslet Road
Leeds LS10 1JW, England

ISBN 0 903805 08 1

Printed by Regent (Printers) Ltd., 29 Leathley Road, Leeds LS10 1BG.    Tel. (0532) 21404

# Preface

This collection of word studies if offered to Bible students as a sequel to *The Greatest Old Testament Words* (1964) and follows the same general arrangement.

The transliteration of words follows Robert Young's *Analytical Concordance to the Bible* (Eighth edit.1939).

The emphasis is again laid on the use made of words in their varying context rather than on their etymologies.

A number of the studies have appeared as contributions to *The Congregational Monthly* and *The Church Teacher* and I am grateful to the editors of these journals for their permission to use the material in this form.

Professor William Barclay who contributed a preface to the first collection of studies has once again put me in his debt by reading the manuscript of the present study and contributing a foreword.

**Edgar Jones**

# Contents

# Introduction

I  CONCERNING GOD

1. The Names of God ... ... ... ... ... ... ... 13
2. God Alive ... ... ... ... ... ... ... ... 17
3. God the Creator ... ... ... ... ... ... ... 21
4. The Wrath of God ... ... ... ... ... ... ... 25
5. The Grace of God ... ... ... ... ... ... ... 29
6. God the Judge ... ... ... ... ... ... ... ... 33
7. The God Who Makes Room ... ... ... ... ... 37

II  CONCERNING MAN

8. In the Image of God ... ... ... ... ... ... ... 43
9. The Imagination of Man ... ... ... ... ... ... 47
10. The Prophetic Paradox ... ... ... ... ... ... 51
11. God's Elect ... ... ... ... ... ... ... ... 55
12. The Joy of The Lord ... ... ... ... ... ... ... 59
13. The Love that Elects ... ... ... ... ... ... ... 63
14. God — Our next of kin ... ... ... ... ... ... 67

III  CONCERNING CULT AND COMMUNITY

15. The Sabbath ... ... ... ... ... ... ... ... 73
16. The Power of the Poor ... ... ... ... ... ... 77
17. God's Strangers ... ... ... ... ... ... ... ... 81
18. The Way of the Lord ... ... ... ... ... ... ... 85
19. The Ark — Furniture or Faith? ... ... ... ... ... 91
20. Remember Tomorrow! ... ... ... ... ... ... 95
21. The Year of the Trumpet ... ... ... ... ... ... 99

READING LIST ... ... ... ... ... ... ... ... 103

# Introduction

Interpreting the Bible is a responsible undertaking and anyone who would venture upon it is faced with a number of tasks.

## *The task of discovering what the Bible says*

This is not as easy as it sounds. In translation from one language to another there is inevitably some loss. For example, the Hebrew word for 'peace' (shalom) means much more than just not fighting! Prosperity, well-being, security, welfare are all part of the original idea and even then it is not exhausted. Another factor in estimating this first task is the difficulty in finding out what the original text was. Because of the nature of the transmission through centuries of copying by the scribes it is inevitable that there are mistakes. Already because of the discovery of the Dead Sea Scrolls text of Isaiah, the R.S.V. is able to use some fifteen different readings that give us a more accurate translation. Similarly, the interpreter must be able to distinguish between prose and poetry, history and parable. Neither the story of the Fall in Genesis, chapter 3, nor the story of Jonah and the Whale were intended as actual history, but their *truth* is far beyond mere historical fact of the 1066 variety!

## The task of re-creating the life-situation

The second need of the interpreter is to enter imaginatively into the original setting of the Bible passage. This makes demands upon mind and spirit. An exile or refugee reading Isaiah 40 or 53 would know what it was all about. Hosea is meaningful at its deepest level from within the experience of a home breaking up and the wonderful experience of reconciliation. The parallel of the underground movements of the last war offer a key to understanding the Book of Daniel, which is virtually a resistance document. There is an imperative need to enter into the experience of the Bible speaker and sit where he has sat!

## The task of discovering the direction of the Bible passage

Every Bible passage has, as it were, an arrow pointing forward or backward. There is an act of God that it points to or an act of God from which it is derived. The great creative moments of God's dealing with his people are the Exodus, the Exile, the Incarnation, the Crucifixion and the Resurrection. So for example when Job asks wistfully: 'If a man die, shall he live again?' such a passage points forward like an arrow to the Easter message where alone the question is answered. Similarly, when Paul affirms: 'No, in all these things we are more than conquerors through him who loved us,' we know that the arrow or direction of this passage points back to the experience of the Risen Lord. So with all the great 'moments' of the Bible story. Every Bible passage can be interpreted through asking what does it point forward to, or from what does this insight or teaching stem?

## The task of finding the personal centre of the Bible

Modern Bible interpretation demands that we see the progressive revelation of God's purpose in it and indeed so often the Bible corrects itself. For example, the savage imprecations of part of Psalm 58 or Psalm 137 must also be assessed against the teaching of the Sermon on the Mount. The issue is — how do we select the standard by which various parts of the Bible are judged? Must it be an individual whim? Not at all. The lowest must be judged in terms of the highest, and the greatest insight the Bible affords is that of the purpose of God revealed through Christ, crucified on the Cross and risen from the dead. All that does not match up to this standard — his expressed mind must then be regarded as secondary and subordinate. We must note that the centre of the Bible in terms of which all else is to be judged is not a proposition but a personal relationship.

## The task of communicating the life behind the language

Behind the Biblical terms and thought-form there is a life to be communicated. We must beware of a fundamentalism not only of belief in a literal text that is infallible, but of using terms that are meaningless to us and belong to another world. Yet there is the living truth of that day that cries to be expressed in terms of today. For example, what does redemption mean? To Paul, a Hebrew, the Old Testament function of one who redeems or releases a slave in the market place is just a picture of the wonderful experience of being free after being a slave. This is what it means to be a Christian and redeemed. To be meaningful today, we may have to use the sense of liberation that people have known coming from Eastern Germany over the Wall, or the sense of being freed from the mass production system that to many is felt as a slavery of the mind and heart in a gadget civilisation. Whatever the terms used, the life behind is the thing that counts, and each generation must find the comparable experience that releases the life behind the language

After these five tasks of the interpreter what more is to be said? Just this, that all such approach to interpretation demands even more *the acceptance of personal involvement*. The Bible cannot be interpreted from the outside. To understand what the Bible says about prayer and forgiveness it is first of all necessary to feel the need of prayer and to get on one's knees. All Bible interpretation at the deepest level demands a living relationship with God. Let us make the call of William Neil our own: "We must attempt to steer a middle course between a fruitless effort to reinstate Bible words and ideas which are now merely relics of the past, and the equally profitless and more dangerous endeavour to lose contact with the historical basis and restate the Bible in the terminology of Marx or Freud or the Existentialists. Nor is there anything to be gained by the cry, 'Back to the Reformers.' If we believe at all in the power of the Spirit . . . we cannot allow that he has less to say to today than to past ages, or that he cannot say it in the language of our time."

# 1 Concerning God

# 1. The Names of God

As we begin our study of the significance of the words of the Old Testament we may fittingly start with the very ones used for God himself. We do this not because of some sense of completeness but because one of the characteristics of Hebrew thought is that name and nature of a person are closely related. The name is considered as a revelation of the owner's nature and personality. We see this emphasis on the name in two passages. First in the Priestly Blessing: "The Lord bless thee, and keep thee: the Lord make his face shine upon thee, and be gracious unto thee: the Lord lift up his countenance upon thee, and give thee peace. And they shall put my name upon the children of Israel; and I will bless them" (Numbers 6.24-27). Similarly, in the Psalter we read: The Lord answer you in the day of trouble. The Name of the God of Jacob protect you! (Ps.20.1).

We shall look briefly at three of the most significant names given to God in the Old Testament.

## Elohim

This is the term that is translated 'God.' The original form is *'el* but it is found some 2,500 times in the plural. In the same language family we have *ilu* in Akkadian and *allah* in Arabic. Behind this term there are two basic ideas. First, the *idea of force and strength* that we find illustrated in the scene that described Laban after he confronts Jacob with his trickery: "It is in my power to do you harm; but the God of your Father spake to me last night saying: 'Take heed that you speak to Jacob neither good nor bad " (Gen. 31.9 and see also Deut. 28.32; Prov. 3.27; Micah 2.1; Neh. 5.5). The phrase 'in my power' is literally 'in the *el* of my hand.' Secondly, the same root is used with the meaning of being in the forefront, at the head. So we find the word *'avil*, the one at the head of the flock, is the word for ram and the consonants are the same as *'el* — God. The central ideas contained in Elohim — God — are those of pre-eminence and power. God is the first and he possesses all force. This linking of deity and dynamic is the source of our growing realization that God is a God who acts!

*Yahweh*

This name is more familiar to many of us as Jehovah in the A.V. and as Lord in the R.V. Actually, all we know of a certainty are the Hebrew consonants YHWH and the vowels that have been added are those of the Hebrew term for 'master.' This is a sort of linguistic camouflage to avoid uttering the Divine name on grounds of reverence. The precise origin of Yahweh is not too clear but it is certainly connected with the verb *hawah* to be. The central passage for our consideration is found in Exodus 3.14: "And Moses said unto God, Behold, when I come unto the children of Israel, and shall say unto them, The God of your fathers hath sent me to you; and they shall say to me, What is his name? what shall I say unto them? And God said unto Moses, I AM THAT I AM: and he said, Thus shalt thou say unto the children of Israel, I AM hath sent me unto you". The answer is not really a rebuff for Moses but an affirmation that God is alive and vital. This has been admirably expressed in a recent comment, " *'El* expresses life in its power, *Yahweh* expresses life in its continuance and its actuality, *Yahweh* is indeed he who is." (Jacob, *Theology of the Old Testament*, p.51). One of the striking characteristics of God that we find from the use of the name Yahweh is that it is used of God as one who *is essentially in relationship with his people*. The following passages illustrate this feature.

Moses hesitates to go to Pharaoh and plead for the release of his people but God reassures him: "And he said, certainly I will be with thee; and this shall be a token unto thee, that I have sent thee: when thou hast brought forth the people out of Egypt, ye shall serve God upon this mountain" (Exod. 3.12).

Again, Gideon is commissioned by God to free the Israelites from the power of Midian and protests that his clan is the weakest and he himself the youngest in the family but God answers: "And the angel of the Lord appeared unto him, and said unto him, the Lord is with thee, thou mighty man of valour" (Judges 6.12).

*Yahweh* is always with his people and this in two ways.

*Yahweh is present in judgment.* "I will judge them; and they shall know that I am *Yahweh*" (Ezek. 7.27 and see also 6.13; 11.10; and 12.16). In the same book we read also that Yahweh is present with promise: "And you shall know that I am *Yahweh* when I open your graves, and raise you from your graves, O my people" (Exek. 37-13).

### *Lord of Hosts*

A final name given to God and found some 279 times is that of Lord of Hosts — *Yahweh of Tsebaoth.* We find it used in such passages as "Even the Lord, the God of Hosts; the Lord is his memorial" (Hosea 12.15). "Oh Lord God of Hosts, who is a mighty one, like unto thee, O Jah" (Ps. 89.9).

Three suggestions have been made as to the meaning of this title given to God. It might refer to the earthly forces of the Israelite armies or the hosts of the celestial bodies, or even the heavenly forces of spirits thought to reside in the stars. A recent comment has been that "the prophets saw in the use of the expression a polemical point directed against the spread of the cult of the stars and of the spirits which were thought to animate them, and in the face of which it had to be affirmed that *Yahweh* was the only lord of the army of the heavens."

The underlying affirmation is that the Lordship of God is total — there is One God! We see that to call God by his names is a significant activity — it is to affirm one's credo. God is First and Foremost! God is a Living God. God is God alone. God is with his people to judge and to redeem. All this and more lies behind the Names of God.

15

# 2. God Alive

At a time when many greatly exaggerated and indeed premature reports are heard of the Death of God, it is reassuring to look again at this central affirmation of the Bible. Again and again, the phrase recurs 'the Living God' ('elohim chai). Behind this triumphant claim there are at least four trumpet notes to be heard.

### The Living God acts in History

In the early stories of the struggles of the Hebrews we have a picture of God as a direct participant in their battles, indeed the architect of the nation's victories (Josh. 3.10). The same note is heard in the experience of Isaiah as he describes the Siege of Jerusalem by Sennecherib. Rabshakeh, the Assyrian commander, has contemptuously taunted Hezekiah, with the boast that no other gods have ever delivered other nations, so why should there be an exception now? "Who among all the gods of these countries have delivered their countries out of my hand, that the Lord should deliver Jerusalem out of my hand?" (Isa. 36.20). The prophet assures the king that there is a door that is open, a door of hope. "It may be that the Lord your God heard the words of the Rabshakeh, whom his master the king of Assyria has sent to mock the Living God, and he will rebuke the words which the Lord your God has heard; therefore lift up your prayer for the remnant that is left." (Isa. 37.4). The Living God is no spectator deity on the touch-line. Because he is the Living God he must enter into the living of these days. The Hebrew phrase (chai) means not only that God exists but that He acts. It stands for his presence and his power.

17

## The Living God offers a Living Relationship

From the field of battle we come to the courts of the Temple to meet the Living God in the realm of praise and prayer. We hear an exile, who has himself led pilgrims in procession to the Temple sanctuary, cry out: "As a hart longs for flowing streams, so longs my soul for thee, O God, for the Living God. When shall I come and behold the face of God? My tears have been my food day and night, while men say to me continually, 'Where is your God?' " (Ps. 42 2-3). Here beyond the noise of battle, a deeper note is sounded. The Living God not only intervenes in history but he shares the living relationship that is the heart of worship. This need is gloriously fulfilled in the experience of a fellow-psalmist who exclaims: "How lovely is thy dwelling place, O Lord of Hosts! My soul longs, yea, faints for the courts of the Lord; my heart and flesh sing for joy to the Living God." (Ps. 84-2).

## The Living God is the Source of Life

The experience of the Living God gathers momentum. Not only is God Alive — he is the source of all life. The contrast between the Living God and the dead gods is seen in such a scathing picture of a natural break in an idol factory in Babylon, with the men gathered around their end-product: "Everyone helps his neighbour, and says to his brother, 'Take courage!' The craftsman encourages the goldsmith, and he who smooths with the hammer, him who strikes the anvil, saying of the soldering, 'It is good'; and they fasten it with nails so that it cannot be moved." (Isa. 41. 6-7; see also Isa. 40. 18-20; Isa. 44. 12-17; Jer. 10. 3-5). In contrast, the Living God is the well-spring of life although his people may not always realize this. In Jeremiah's poignant words, "They have forsaken me, the fountain of living waters, and hewed out cisterns for themselves, broken cisterns that can hold no water." (Jer. 2.13; see John 4.14). Yet when he comes to himself, the supreme goal of the Hebrew is to be bound up "in the bundle of life" with the Living God (1 Sam. 25.29).

## The Living God is the guarantee of Life Eternal

The affirmation that God is a Living God points beyond the Old Testament and reaches its consummation in the Incarnation and the Resurrection. From the Letter of Hope, a voice in the Early Church speaks: "Come to him, to that living stone, rejected by men in God's sight chosen and precious; and like living stones be yourselves built into a spiritual house, to be a holy priesthood, to offer spiritual sacrifices acceptable to God through Jesus Christ." (1 Pet. 4-5). And again he speaks, "Blessed be the God and Father of our Lord Jesus Christ! By his great mercy we have been born anew to a living hope through the resurrection of Jesus Christ from the dead." (1 Pet. 1.3). It is no accident that in time of stress and trial the emphasis is laid on men and women being *living* stones of a spiritual temple because their foundation and guarantee is their *living hope* of the Resurrection Faith. God Alive! In History, in human relationships, the source of all life here and now and the guarantee of Life Eternal!

# 3. The Creator God

"In the beginning God created . . . " (Gen. 1.1). The Bible starts with this majestic affirmation. There is no tentative enquiry as to whether this might be so, but the certainty of a man who knows. Yet this certainty is the result of a great spiritual adventure. The word translated 'created' is the root *bara'* and in the instances of the verb being used the subject is invariably God. It is God alone who can create. Men may form and fashion but the Creator is God alone.

In the Bible we may select four main emphases in its teaching concerning creation, the unique act of the unique God.

## Creator because Redeemer

The faith of the Bible concerning God as creator does not spring from man's speculation concerning the origin of things but it is the direct outcome of the experience of having been delivered, redeemed.

In Exodus 20.2 we read:

> I am the Lord your God, who brought you out of the land of Egypt, out of the house of bondage."

Here is the central experience that is the core of the certainty about God the Creator. It is because God is the one who has redeemed or delivered his people that the Hebrew writer can find only one answer to the question — Who created the world? Who else could it be but the one who has delivered them from oppression and tyranny. This insight is reinforced as we read the early credos in Deut. 26.5f. or Josh. 24. 3-8.

21

And you shall make response before the Lord your God, A wandering Aramean was my father; and he went down into Egypt and sojourned there, few in number . . . Then we cried to the Lord the God of our fathers, and the Lord heard our voice, and saw our affliction, our toil, our oppression; and the Lord brought us out of Egypt with a mighty hand. (Deut. 26. 5-8).

It is significant that no mention is made in these early forms of a credo, of any belief in God as Creator. It is because of the experience of deliverance and redemption from Egypt that the Hebrew mind could find no other answer to the question Who is the Creator of heaven and earth? It could only be the One who Redeems Israel:

This says the Lord, your Redeemer, the Holy One of Israel: "For your sake I will send to Babylon and break down all the bars, and the shouting of the Chaldeans will be turned into lamentations. I am the Holy One, the Creator of Israel, your King" (Isa. 43. 14-15, see also v.24 and Isa. 45.7; 40.21f.).

In such passages the return from the Exile is heralded as another Exodus, and the nation is re-created through another act of God's redeeming power.


## Creation and Covenant

If we ask why did God create the world the answer of the Bible is quite clear — to express and fulfil his Covenant Love. The initiative is always with God and his purpose is to redeem mankind through his chosen instrument, the Chosen People.

Some of the terms used to describe God as creator are master-builder (Job. 38.4-6); or a potter (Jer. 18.1-6) but supremely the unique word used is *bara'* — to create. "In the beginning God created . . . " (Gen. 1.1). The verb never has any other subject than God and the object of this verb *bara'*, is never a substance as in an intermediate stage, but always refers to the completed, perfect work. The word expresses absolute sovereignty. God is the Unique Creator not some middleman or manufacturer of gods. This uniqueness is expressed above all in the Covenant Relationship. This central purpose of Creation is seen in a number of Bible passages. When through human sin it seems God's purpose is being obstructed, it is striking that after the account of the Flood the commands of the Creation Story of Genesis 1.28 are now repeated within a covenant context despite the sins of men:

> And you be fruitful and multiply, bring forth abundantly on the earth, and multiply in it (Gen. 9.7) . . .

> And God said to Noah and to his sons with him, "Behold, I establish my covenant with you and your descendants after you" (Gen. 9.7-8).

No rebellion of men may ever hold up God's purpose in Creation, to redeem his people through a Covenant relationship.

A further link between Creation and Covenant is seen in the writings of Second Isaiah, when he interprets what the experience of Exile means to his people, although such an experience of desolation appears to put an end to God's purpose:

> Thus says God, the Lord, who created the heavens and stretched them out, who spread forth the earth and what comes from it . . . I am the Lord, I have called you in righteousness, I have taken you by the hand and kept you; I have given you as a covenant to the people a light to the nations (Isa. 42.5-6).

The experience of being in exile, separated from the Temple and the Homeland leads the people to see that this is the purpose of being created God's Chosen, Elect people, that they might be used to extend the Covenant relationship to the rest of the world. The act of creation intends to bring the whole of mankind into covenant relationship with God, this is what Creation is about.


*Creation and New Creation*

The fullest expression of a new creation is seen in the New Testament in such passages as:

> Therefore, if any one is in Christ, he is a new creation; the old one has passed away, behold, the new has come (2 Cor. 5.17).

> For we are his workmanship, created in Christ Jesus for good works, which God prepared beforehand, that we should walk in them (Ephes. 2.10).

The audacity of these claims needs to be underlined. The purpose of God's original creation is that men should share in the covenant love shown supremely in Jesus Christ. Beyond the nationalistic and physical definition of the old Israel, we now have the new re-created Israel, the living church which is the reason for God's first creation. Creation reaches its real meaning when men are re-created spiritually:

But to all who receive him, who believed in his name, he gave power to become children of God; who were born, not of blood nor of the will of the flesh nor of the will of man, but of God (John 1.13), (see 5.5).

## *Creation and Consummation*

What the Creator starts he must complete. There can be no unfinished business. The Creator God must achieve his covenant purpose: Therefore before the record closes the testimony must be borne:

> Then I saw a new heaven and a new earth; for the first heaven and the first earth had passed away, and the sea was no more . . . (Rev. 21.1).

To the Eastern mind the sea had undertones of the struggle of God the Creator who had vanquished the Chaos monster at the dawn of creation. Evil was defeated at the outset. The transcendance of evil is the purpose of creation and so we rejoice at the affirmation coming from a time of crisis and tension:

> Behold, I make all things new . . . it is done! I am the Alpha and the Omega, the beginning and the end. To the thirsty I will give water without price from the fountain of the water of life. He who conquers shall have this heritage, and I will be his God and he shall be my son (Rev. 21.5-7).

The new creation and its consummation finds expression once again in the words of the Covenant relationship between God and Man.

It is fitting that those around the throne should sing:

> Worthy art thou, our Lord and God,
> to receive glory and honour and power,
> for thou didst create all things,
> and by thy will they existed and were created (Rev. 4.11).

# 4. The Wrath of God

A strange and disturbing fact that is part of the Old Testament picture of God is the complete realism with which it speaks of the Wrath of God. This is not because they attribute to God the same passions that they have and when they use the phrase 'Wrath of God' they envisage the Lord of Heaven and Earth losing his temper. But they wish to portray God in his entirety, his wholeness. It is actually factually the case, that the terms for anger *'ap* — literally nose and *chemah* — heat are used four times more frequently of God than of man. One phrase, *charon 'ap* — heat of anger, is used only of God. Clearly, the Wrath of God is no casual or colourful way of talking about God but represents a reality of their experience rather than the same human projection upon God of what they had endured in their own history.

The biblical thought concerning the Wrath of God may be crystallized in four affirmations:

*His Wrath is part of His Mystery*

In a number of passages we find that the ancient Israelites saw no major problem in speaking of the wrath of God but accepted it as part of the mystery of God's person and activity. So we read of Uzzah who tried to steady the ark: "And when they came to the threshing floor of Nacon, Uzzah put out his hand to the ark of God and took hold of it, for the oxen stumbled. And the anger of the Lord was kindled against

Uzzah; and God smote him there because he put forth his hand to the ark; and he died there beside the ark of God." (2 Samuel 6.6-7). There is no discussion on the fairness or justice of this, just the recording of a mysterious, irrational act. (see also Exodus 4.24; Genesis 16.13; Judges 13.22; 1 Samuel 6.19). This wrath is in part to be seen as the aspect of the holiness of God which radically separates the creature from the Creator.

## His Wrath is part of His Covenant Relationship

The occasion of God's wrath is primarily that of attempting to thwart his will and purpose to save men, that is, any action that threatens his covenant act. "Take heed lest your heart be deceived, and you turn aside and serve other gods and worship them, and the anger of the Lord be kindled against you." (Deuteronomy 11.16-17). Joshua reaffirms the words of Moses: "If you transgress the covenant of the Lord your God — then the anger of the Lord will be kindled against you" (Joshua 23.16 and see also Deuteronomy 12.23; 13.19; 29.15-19; Ezekiel 5.13; 16.38; 36.6).

There is another side to this relationship between the wrath of God and his covenant with his people. If the breaking of the covenant by the people provokes the anger of God, yet God's faithfulness to the covenant he has himself initiated, also constrains his anger. Thus we read of the dilemma and conflict of God himself. "How can I give you up. O Ephraim, How can I hand you over, O Israel — My heart recoils within me, my compassion grows warm and tender. I will not execute my fierce anger, I will not again destroy Ephraim; for I am God and not man, the Holy One in your midst, and I will not come to destroy." (Hosea 11.8-9) see also Exodus 32.10; 12-14; Psalm 103.8; Isaiah 54.7-8, 10; Micah 7.18.

## He offers Salvation from His Wrath

There are two main ways in which men may be saved from the wrath of God in the Old Testament. First, through the *ritual of the cult*, "but the Levites shall encamp around the tabernacle of the testimony, that there may be no wrath upon the congregation of the people of Israel; and the Levites shall keep charge of the tabernacle of the testimony."

(Numbers 1.53). Secondly, men may be saved from God's anger when they *repent (return)* of their breaking of the covenant relationship. This note is heard again and again in the prophetic books. So Jeremiah pleads, "It may be that their supplication will come before the Lord, and that every one will turn from his evil way, for great is the anger and wrath that the Lord has pronounced against this people." (Jeremiah 36.7; see also Jeremiah 4.4; Amos 5.15: 3.7.16).

Yet God is so anxious that men should return that he himself will carry out the necessary conditions or send a messenger to bring about the change of heart. "And they shall be my people, and I will be their God. I will give them one heart and one way, that they may fear me for ever." (Jeremiah 32.38-39; Deuteronomhy 30.6; Ezekiel 36.26-27). And again the initiative of God in saving men from his own wrath is seen in such a passage as: "Behold, I will send you Elijah the prophet before the great and terrible day of the Lord comes. And he will turn the hearts of fathers to their children and the hearts of children to their fathers, lest I come and smite the land with a curse." (Malachi 4.5-6).

## The Wrath of God has an End

As the Old Testament ended with the prophecy of God's messenger bringing about a change of heart in mankind so the New Testament reaffirms the note of hope — *that God's last word is not his word of anger.* This is not to say that God's judgment of sin or his wrath at its continuance now becomes facile or cheap. Such a passage as the following shatters such naive optimism: "Fall on us and hide us from the face of him, who is seated on the throne, and from the wrath of the Lamb:" (Revelations 6.16; see also John 3.36; Romans 1.17-18). Yet the Love of God outlasts his wrath. So we have first, a hope of reconciliation: "For God has not destined us for wrath, but to obtain salvation through our Lord Jesus Christ" (1 Thessalonians 5.9). Finally, beyond hope, certainty. "Behold, the dwelling of God is with men. He will dwell with them, and they shall be his people, and God himself will be with them; he will wipe away every tear from their eyes, and death shall be no more, neither shall there be mourning nor crying nor pain any more, for the former things have passed away" (Revelations 21.3-4).

So we end where we started. The breaking of the Covenant provokes the Wrath of God and God's final act of reaffirming the Covenant will end his wrath and proclaim his continuing love.

# 5. The Grace of God

If one had to choose one word to express the heart of the Bible story one could make a strong case for the word 'Grace'. Indeed both Old and New Testaments might not be unfairly summarised by this term in all it presupposes and all it promises. This present study is concerned primarily with the Old Testament words *chen* and *chanun* — grace and gracious.

The original meaning of the root from which they come was 'to bend, bow or incline.' As the physical action of bending and inclining is involved in the bestowing of a favour or a condescension we can readily see the development of the central idea of *chen* being used to express some aspect of the relationship between a superior and an inferior. What is always absent in the 67 or so instances of *chen* is any idea of equality, of being a relationship between equals. For example, the phrase 'to find favour *(chen)* in the sight of' occurs some 43 times.

The word is used in the first place of ordinary human relationships. The sons of Reuben and Gad speak to Moses requesting permission to settle in Gilead: "And they said, 'If we have found favour in your sight, let this land be given to your servant for a possession'" (Numbers 32.5). So in laws concerning the releasing of slaves we read: "When you buy a Hebrew slave, he shall serve six years, and in the seventh he shall go out free, for nothing" (Exodus 21.2). Here the adverbial form is used *chinnam* and is equivalent to our gratis, for nothing. There must be no backlash. The superior owner must say to the inferior one, the slave — You are free!

We may crystallize the Biblical teaching contained in the use of *chen* and chanun, grace and gracious in four affirmations.

## Grace represents the Sovereign Act of God

The first significant fact to be noted is that in no passage where God reveals his grace or is said to be gracious, is there any suggestion of such an action being earned or deserved. An example is found in Exodus 22: "If ever you take your neighbour's garment in pledge, you shall restore it to him before the sun goes down; for that is his only covering, it is his mantle for his body; in what else shall he sleep? And if he cries to me, I will hear, for I am *chanun* (gracious)" (vv.26-27). This is much more than the Revised Standard Version rendering 'compassionate.' What God is saying is that it does not matter whether the one who has given his garment in pledge is righteous or whether he has been an indifferent ne'er do well tramp. His need and cry for help is all that matters. There is nothing here about the deserving or undeserving destitute only the nature of God in being gracious to all and sundry who will accept.

So too does God deal with the nation. A passage from the prophets illustrates this recurring gracious note. In Isaiah 30 we have domination of the political intrigues of the pro-Egyptian party and an exposure of the futility of political alliance. This is followed by a picture of an ideal future for those faithful remnants who have survived the judgment upon the idolatrous State:

"Therefore the Lord waits to be gracious to you; therefore he exalts himself to show mercy to you. For the Lord is a God of justice; blessed are all these who wait for him. Yea, O people in Zion who dwell at Jerusalem; you shall weep no more. He will surely be gracious to you at the sound of your cry; when he hears it, he will answer you" (Isaiah 30.18-19; see also Amos 5.15; Jeremiah 31.2; Zechariah 4.7).

## Grace and Man's Response

A parallel feature to the gracious action of God in the Old Testament is the evident consciousness of being in need of it, both individual and nation. So Moses, at the Tent of Meeting where God used to speak to him as a man speaks to his friend, speaks with a deep passionately felt concern: "See, thou sayest to me, 'Bring up this people;' but thou hast not let me know whom thou wilt send with me. Yet hast thou said, 'I know you by name, and you have also found grace *(chen)* in thy sight, show me now thy ways, that I may know thee and find grace in thy sight, I and thy people? Is it not in thy going with us, so that we are distinct, I and thy people, from all other people that are upon the face of the earth?' " (Exodus 33.12-16).

Clearly Moses felt quite inadequate to face the wilderness journey to the Promised Land unless he and his people are assured that God is ready to give his grace to them. In such a passage we see underlined the awareness of the need of grace. It is this awareness of need that is the heart of man's response to the gracious acts of God.

## Grace and Righteousness

A striking feature of the use of *chanun* (gracious) which is used only of God some 13 times, is that in all but three of those there is a reference to God judging the very people who have experienced his grace. The God who is gracious may never be completely divorced from the God who is righteous.

This is well illustrated in the account of Moses before God on Sinai, receiving the tablets of stone. "The Lord passed before him, and proclaimed, 'The Lord, the Lord, a God merciful and gracious, *(chanun)*, slow to anger, and abounding in steadfast love and faithfulness, keeping steadfast love for thousands, forgiving iniquity and transgression and sin, but who will by no means clear the guilty, visiting the iniquity of the fathers upon the children, to the third and the fourth generation'." (Exodus 34.6-8).

The grace of God must never be equated with some casual attitude to human sin. It does matter and cost. Yet God's righteousness never invalidates his grace. A striking example is found in the prophet Joel. He has painted in sombre colours the judgment accompanying the dreaded Day of the Lord and his voice rings out with the challenge: And who can abide it? Yet he must to be true to God and continues:

" 'Yet even now,' says the Lord. 'return to me with all your heart, with fasting, with weeping, and with mourning; and rend your hearts and not your garments.' Return to the Lord, your God, for he is gracious (chanun) and merciful, slow to anger, and abounding in steadfast love, and repents of evil" (Joel 2.12-13).

This is the great paradox that Paul enumerates in his letter to the Ephesians: "For by grace you have been saved through faith; and this is not your own doing, it is the gift of God — not because of works, lest any man should boast" (Ephesians 2.8).

*Christ the Consummation of God's Grace*

Because grace is not a commodity to be dispensed but a relationship which God establishes and within which a man may live in God's presence, the end of God's gracious dealing with men is that he should give himself. Viewed in this light the coming of Christ and the possibly of his indwelling with us, of our being in him is the consummation of all that the grace of God points forward to in the Old Testament. The Fourth Gospel expresses this in words that have rejoiced the heart over the centuries: "And from his fullness have we all received, grace upon grace. For the law was given through Moses; grace and truth came through Jesus Christ" (John 1.16-17). This experience of men in every generation is the justification of the tremendous dawn that is movingly described by William Temple, 'we can say that the word tabernacled among us is full of grace and truth because in our own experience we have drawn upon that treasure store, and have found that the more we drew the more remained that we might also draw from that; for every grace received there was more offered.'

(Readings in St. John's Gospel, 1939, p.16).

# 6. God as Judge

Silence in Court! This would be a fitting introduction to many of the major utterances of the Hebrew prophets. It would even serve as an interpretive key to Biblical thought concerning God and Man. Throughout the Bible God is judging his people. So we have such a court room scene as this: "Hear, you peoples, all of you; hearken, O earth, and all that is in it; and let the Lord God be a witness against you, the Lord from his holy temple" (Micah 1.2). Or again the opening outburst of Isaiah represents a calling for order because God is about to state his case in court. "Hear, O heavens, and give ear, O earth; for the Lord has spoken" (Isaiah 1.2). What follows in both passages is the case for the prosecution delivered by God who is the supreme *shophet* — judge (see also Jer. 2; Job 31.35; Isaiah 41.1 for the court-room motif).

The basic root is *shaphat* (to judge) and from this we have *shophet* (a judge) and *mishpat* — judgement or justice. Yet as we shall see from Old Testament usage the fatal mistake to make is to equate the term 'judge' to what we mean by this legal official procedure. The term 'to judge' in Hebrew thought is much richer and positive and is often parallel to 'to help' and 'to save' (see Isa. 1.17; Ps. 7.6-8; Ps. 26.1). The first reference (Isa. 1.17) casts God as judge and plaintiff and no law court as we know would stand for that! The emphasis in the word *shophet* is upon the idea of conforming to a norm. The very nature of God is that He is just. "Shall not the Judge *(shophet)* of all the earth do right" *(mishpat)* (Gen. 18.25). This is his *mishpat* (nature). This is only expressed when he is revealing his will and purpose. When God judges he is doing far more than giving a verdict or punishing a wrong-doer. He is making a claim upon his people that they live in accordance with his nature.

We may summarise a wealth of theological insight in a number of fundamental principles as we consider what the Bible says about God as Judge.

### God's Judgment presupposes his Covenant

We must immediately remove from our minds any idea of the gloriously impartial figure of justice we usually have. A recent commentator reminds us, 'The justice of Yahweh is not of the type of the blindfolded maiden holding a balance in her hand, the justice of Yahweh extends one arm to the wretch stretched out on the ground whilst the other pushes away the one who causes the misfortune.' God is not impartial. He does take sides and from within the covenant relationship he makes his just demands and judges those who fall short. Yet this is not the administration of abstract principles. Justice pure and simple would be blasphemy for the Hebrew for his God would not be involved. So the psalmist cries: "May he judge the poor of the people and save the children of the needy, and crush the oppressor" (Ps. 72.4). This is what is expected of the ideal king, after God's own heart or *mishpat*. We note that the three parallel ideas are 'judge,' 'save' and 'to crush the oppressor.' This is much more than an edict from the Bench. So in the Prologue of Second Isaiah we read: "Why do you say, O Jacob, and speak, O Israel, My way is hid from the Lord and my right *(mishpat)* is disregarded by God?" (Isa. 40.27). God answers this complaint with the glorious affirmations of vv.28-31. The people are saying that their just claim for consideration by God has not been met. This is the legalistic idea of covenant relationship which God tears down. In effect, he replies, "You have forgotten the dimension of the God of Israel — your God is too small. How dare you talk about your legal right (mishpat)? Have you forgotten your own law, 'you shall not be afraid of the face of man, for the judgment *(mishpat)* is God's' " (Deut. 1.17).

### God's Judgment ensures Victory

A second characteristic of God's judging is that his judgment means victory. So in the early accounts of the settlement in Canaan, the leaders who are called judges are also named 'saviours.' "Whenever the Lord raised up judges (shophetim) for them, the Lord was with the judge, and he saved them from the hands of their enemies all the days of the judge" (Judges 2.18). The same note of victory when God judges is echoed by the psalmists: "When my enemies turned back, they stumbled and perished before thee. For thou hast maintained my just cause (mishpat); thou hast sat in the throne giving righteous judgment" (Ps. 9.3-4, see also Ps. 7.8; Ps. 82.8; 96.13). In this last verse we have the association of two terms that are virtually identical, righteousness and justice, *tsedaqah* and *mishpat*. This identity helps us further to illustrate the link between judgment and victory from the Song of Deborah: 'To the sound of musicians at the watering places, there they repeat the triumphs of the Lord, the triumphs of the peasantry in Israel" (Judges 5.11). The Hebrew for 'triumphs' is 'righteous deeds' which as a parallel means 'acts of judgment or justice.' (See also 1 Sam. 12.7; Ps. 103.6; Micah 6.5). His judgment means victory.

## God's Judgment becomes Justification

The same motif of God as Judge is found throughout the New Testament and especially in Paul's doctrine of justification by faith. The court-room metaphor is the key to such a passage as: "But now the righteousness of God has been manifested apart from the law, although the law and the prophets bear witness to it, the righteousness of God through faith in Jesus Christ for all who believe" (Romans 3.21-22, see also Romans 1.17; 8.34; 2 Cor. 3.9; 11.15). Here Paul, the Hebrew is not forgetting his heritage but using it to express his faith in Christ. He uses the legal terminology just to show its bankruptcy! To talk of being 'put in the right' (the meaning of justification) and 'apart from the law' is to break with the law court and come into the presence of God. This is sheer paradox — the Judge, not hoodwinked for a moment — says to the guilty, this is my judgment — I acquit you! He does not say that the guilty are innocent, but he acquits them all the same (see Luke 19.1-10 and the same attitude of Jesus to Zacchaeus). The essence of justification is that I am judged and found guilty and then acquitted! But this could not happen in a law-court. Yet it happens every day within a covenant relationship — within a family! This is a bringing together again — a reconciling. God in his judging, takes the initiative and justifies me not because of an impersonal law but through the dynamic of his justice, his saving purpose!

As God is my judge, he will restore me to his covenant relationship and gain the victory by joining me in the dock and then lead me out of the court-room to join my fellows in a family gathering — the children of God in the Father's presence.

# 7. The God who makes room

This title is a literal translation of the Hebrew word that is used of God's saving activity. The word, *'moshia,'* (saviour), comes from the root *yasha* which means to be wide, spacious. When God saves his people he makes room for them to develop despite all contrary forces. Salvation is having room enough to live — living room. The Saviour God is the God who makes room.

The term 'Saviour' occurs some thirty two times apart from the occurrences of the root in other forms. From this wealth of material a number of truths emerge to give a picture of the Bible view of God and what his salvation means.

*Salvation means Victory.*

One of the earliest emphases is that of Victory. So in Judges 15.18 we read of Samson's victory over the Philistines — "With the jawbone of an ass have I slain a thousand men — And he was very thirsty, and he called on the Lord and said, 'Thou hast granted this great deliverance *(teshuah)* by the hand of thy servant.'" Similarly, Jonathan is given victory against the Philistines at Michmash. "And Jonathan said to the young man who bore his armour, 'Come, let us go over to the garrison of these uncircumcised; it may be that the Lord will work for us; for nothing can hinder the Lord from saving by many or by few.'" (1 Samuel 14.6).

## Salvation is Positive

In many passages there is clearly a negative aspect to salvation, that is, it is *salvation from*. As in Judges 6.14: "And the Lord turned to him and said, 'Go in this might of yours and deliver (yasha) Israel from the hand of Midian; do not I send you?' " 'In this directive of God to Gideon there is clearly an answer to the Israelites' cry for one who will save them (see v.6). Yet the most significant emphasis in the Hebrew idea of salvation is positive and the word acquires the notes of wholeness of body, victory, freedom. In short the word is used to describe the range of God's activities —this is what he is — the Saviour God. A striking example of this positive emphasis—*a salvation for and salvation from* is seen in Psalm 91. In this psalm we have a well-loved picture of God's power. The demonic forces may wage against the psalmist, plagues may rage yet: "Because he cleaves to me in love, I will deliver him; I will protect him. When he calls to me, I will answer him because he knows my name. I will be with him in trouble, I will rescue him and honour him. With long life I will satisfy him, and show him my salvation (yeshua)" (91.14-16).

The whole of the psalm is summarized in the last word — salvation. The person who commits his life to God finds room to live.

## Salvation Yesterday, Today and Tomorrow

A further characteristic of the Old Testament experience of salvation is that it is affirmed of the past, present and future. The following passages illustrate the tenses of salvation. In the past certainly:

"I am the Lord your God from the land of Egypt; you know no God but me, and besides me there is no saviour. It was I who knew you in the wilderness, in the land of drought." (Hosea 13.4; see 14.4-5) see also Amos 3.2. Yet the main burden of the prophets and especially in Deuteronomy is that the God who saved their fathers was the God who was ready to save them, to offer a salvation today: "Not with our fathers did the Lord make this covenant, but with us, who are all of us here alive this day," (Deuteronomy 5.3; see also 6.20-24). So we come to the link between salvation and the future. From an exile estranged from his homeland comes the message of a salvation that is to come: "When you pass through the waters I will be with you; when you walk through the fire you shall not be burned, and the flame shall not consume you. For I am the Lord your God, the Holy One of Israel, your Saviour"

(Isaiah 42.2-3). Again from Zechariah, of Jerusalem in a New age we read:

"Behold, I will save my people from the east country and from the west country, and I will bring them to dwell in the midst of Jerusalem; and they shall be my people and I will be their God, in faithfulness and in righteousness." (Zechariah 8.7-8).

God is a saving God, Yesterday, Today and Tomorrow (see Hebrews 13.8).

*Salvation and Righteousness*

A fourth feature of salvation in the prophecies of Second Isaiah especially is the close link between salvation and justice. In the prophet a number of passages show salvation to be practically synonymous with justice and righteousness. Such passages are Isaiah 45.8; 46.13; and 51.6,8.

"Shower, O heavens, from above, and let the skies rain down righteousness; let the earth open, that salvation may sprout forth, and let it cause righteousness to spring up also; I the Lord have created it." (Isaiah 45.8). The parallelism between salvation and righteousness here is clear.

Similarly in Isaiah 46.3, we read: "I bring near my righteousness (RSV deliverance) it is not far off, and my salvation will not tarry; I will put salvation in Zion, for Israel my glory." And also in Isaiah 51.5,6: "My righteousness (RSV deliverance) draws near speedily, my salvation has gone forth — but my salvation will be for ever, and my deliverance will never be ended." (see also v.8) (righteousness). The dominant note in such passages is that crystallized in Isaiah 45.21: "Was it not I, the Lord? And there is no other God besides me, a righteous God and a Saviour."

It is quite unwarrantable to make this an Either-Or as if I must choose between a righteous God and a Saviour. It is Both-And. Because of God's Righteousness (the word means norm i.e. his nature) therefore he is a Saviour, not despite his righteousness but because of it, God saves.

## God the Only Saviour

The term 'saviour' ('moshia') is used of the leaders in the early Settlement period, such as applied to Othniel, in the times of the Judges (see Judges 3.9, 15.31) yet it is significant that it is God who raises up these 'saviours.' For the most part the subject of the verb to save is God himself. Without doubt, the Old Testament affirms that Salvation is of the Lord. This is the recurring theme:

"I, I am the Lord, and besides me there is no saviour." (Isaiah 43.11). The same certainty characterizes the cry of the Psalmist: "I thank thee that thou hast answered me and has become my salvation." (Psalm 118.21. — also Psalm 91.16).

Against this background it is not without significance that God's Son should be called Jesus (Yahweh — saves or will save) (Luke 1.31,69) or that he should be greeted with cries of *Hosanna* — *Save us,* we beseech thee (Psalm 118.25; Mt. 21.9).

We still call and He still saves.

# 2 Concerning Man

# 8. In the Image of God

In the image of God. This is an astounding comment on the nature of man. It is all the more significant since it occurs only in the Priestly document that is one of the sources of Genesis, the source that is always stressing the gulf between God and man. This claim on man's behalf is made three times in the Old Testament, Gen. 1. 26,27; Gen. 5.1-3; and Gen 9.6. What does it mean?

*Image of God as representative*

In what does the image consist? Various answers have been given — his upright stature, intelligence, ability to speak, his freedom or spiritual capacity. Yet this is to go too far too quickly.

Two words are used — *tselem (image)* and *demuth* (likeness). They are best seen not as opposites but as complementary. The word translated 'likeness' gives a precision to 'image.' The image is to resemble or be like the original.

In the context, this can only mean man is to be like God (not by any means equal to God). The phrase is best understood against the background of the ancient Near East. It was quite frequent for a king to set up an image in remote provinces of an empire where he would never appear in person. The statue would represent the king and, in the thought of the East, would be the king.

So we frequently meet the Assyrian inscription: 'I will set up my statue in their midst.' The image is the equivalent of an ambassador.

This, then, is the plain meaning of the text: man, that is everyman, not a special kind of man like a king, but the ordinary variety, is the ambassador of God on earth, to represent God to the rest of the universe.

Yet what does the writer seek to convey by such an affirmation? At least three basic facts.

The whole function of the representative is to be able to communicate the mind and will of the one whom he represents. The function of man is to communicate the will and purpose of God. This is the noblest gift that God could give, a gift that is fully seen in the Incarnation, but which in part God has already given to every man.

### Image of God involves Communion

As God's revelation continued, he showed more and more of his will and purpose through psalmist and prophet. As man responded, the image of God became progressively realized. Man was sharing in communion with God.

One of the best expressions of this communion between God and man is found in Psalm viii: "What is man that thou art mindful of him, and the son of man that thou dost care for him? Yet thou hast made him little less than God, and dost crown him with glory and honour."

### Image of God — result in a Commissioning

It is not accidental that both in Genesis 1.27 and also Psalm 8.6, which is a commentary on the earlier passage, the writer passes immediately from affirming that God has given this gift to man, of being made in his image, to a commissioning:

"And let them have dominion over the fish of the sea, and over the birds of the air, and over all the earth, and over every creeping thing that creeps upon the earth" (Fen. 1.26).

The Psalmist's commentary is: "Thou hast given him dominion over the works of thy hands; thou hast put all things under his feet" (Ps. 8.6-8).

The commission to rule, to have dominion, is not the essence of being in the image of God. In the way that man exercises his power to rule, the image of God will be expressed or diminished.

There is no suggestion of an invitation to become Herrenvolk in relation to God's world. Rather, the dominion over creation will be effective as the relationship between God and man deepens and the 'image of God' seen more clearly. Man is commissioned for power but it is derived power and must be rededicated to the Giver and his creation. It is, in the end, power on behalf of, not power over.

### Image of God is Ever Renewed

So far in this brief study we have looked only at the key passage, Gen. 1.26-27. The other two references, Gen. 5.1-3 and 9.6, in on sense add little, being only references back.

Yet there is a tremendous significance in the precise context of these later passages: "This is the book of the generations of Adam. When God created man, he made him in the likeness of God" (Gen. 5.1).

But this could only be written after the account of Genesis chapter 3 with the description of man's alienation from God and his expulsion from Eden. Yet the writer retains the reference to the likeness of God.

Similarly, in Gen. 9.6, we read: "Whoever sheds the blood of man, by man shall his blood be shed; for God made man in his own image."

After the spiritual experiences represented by fall and flood, the image of God is not said to be destroyed. This means that 'the image of God' in man was never intended to suggest a state of perfect rightness. Rather, that God has called man into a relationship with himself.

This is the continuing vocation of man — to be the image of God. Sin is real, but does not cancel automatically this relationship, since it rests on God's will and grace. The image of God continues because God wills it.

In the Book of Wisdom, a final comment is made: "For God created man for incorruption, and made him in the image of his own eternity" (2.23). This points forward to the climax of the ible affirmation about man and the image of God — he is re-created in his image in Christ (Eph. 2.10).

In summary, the Bible speaks about man — everyman — and says: he is the representative of God. He has communion with God and is commissioned to handle the power of God. Sin impairs but never removes the image of God. It is the continuing image and in Christ is ever freshly minted!

# 9. The Imagination of Man

"The Lord saw that the wickedness of man was great in the earth, and that every imagination of the thoughts of his heart was only evil continually." (Gen.6.5). What is this imagination of man that keeps getting him into such trouble?

The Hebrew word translated 'imagination' is *yetzer* and our first need is to distinguish between earlier and later English meanings of the term 'imagination' and also between eastern and western ways of thought.

When the A.V. was produced the idea of imagination was equivalent to the idea of plotting or devising evil. So we have:

Why do the heathen rage, and the people imagine a vain thing? (Ps.2.1).

The Hebrew word carries a meaning of conspiring and so the RSV is much more accurate when it renders the verse:

Why do the nations conspire, and the people plot in vain?

We see that this use of 'imagination' bears no relationship at all to the current view of imagination as 'mental faculty forming images of external objects not present to the senses.' Even more does the original Hebrew differ from our way of thinking. To the ancient Hebrew thought or mental activity had no separate existence. To think was to think what to do next! The essential emphasis is on thought as a preparation for action.

In three of the five instances in which *yetzer* occurs in the Old Testament it is clearly linked with action and evil action at that (see Gen.6.8; Gen.8.21 and Deut.31.21) whilst in two late passages the sense may be good or at least neutral. The significance of the term lies in the way in which it develops in its usage resulting in far-reaching consequences for our interpretation of the Bible and the impact of the Gospel upon the human situation.

We can summarise the main teaching behind *yetzer* (A.V. imagination) in three basic principles.

## Man has a built-in tendency to disintegrate

The word is used to describe what has been called the tendency towards chaos or disintegration that is demonstrably evident in the early accounts of man and his relationships found in the Genesis narratives. So we find a break-up of the relationship between God and man:

> I heard the sound of thee in the garden and I was afraid because I was naked and I hid myself (Gen.3.10).

So, too, the relationship between man and woman begins to come apart when man hides behind a technicality when he lamely tells God that in any case it was the woman who actually took the fruit and gave it to him! (Gen.3.12). We are not, then, surprised that a man should disclaim all responsible relationship and shout defiantly to his Maker, 'Am I my brother's keeper?' This is what is behind the term yetzer, a bias or impulse towards evil. It is significant that this impulse or tendency is attributed to man not merely after the spiritual experience of a Fall but as part of the human lot. This is essential human behaviour —man is created so — he tends to rebel, this is his bias! We find this in the prophet Jeremiah who has no illusions about the natural goodness of man:

> The heart is deceitful about all things, and desperately corrupt; who can understand it? (Jer.17.9; also Jer.16.12;18.12).

What is significant at this stage is that this 'congenital propensity for evil' stems from man's creation, not any seduction by the serpent (for this later view see Sirach 25.24). The psalmist joins the prophet:

> Behold, I was brought forth in iniquity, and in sin did my mother conceive me (Ps.51.5; see also Job.4.17-18).

## The Doctrine of the Two Impulses

One of the major difficulties that arose from the belief in the evil impulse (A.V. imagination) as part of man's endowment at creation was the question of responsibility for sin. Was the will of man inherently sinful so that he had no chance? Judaism would not admit this and in later thought we have the teaching that the Law adhered to faithfully would be enough to resist the evil impulse. So in the apocryphal book the Wisdom of Solomon we read:

> Wisdom protected the first-formed father of the world, when he alone had been created; she delivered him from his transgression (10.1).

Wisdom in apocryphal thought had become equated with the Law (Sirach 24.23). This means that the Law was powerful enough to save Adam from his fall! Again in support of this we read in IV Ezra that the onus for wrongdoing is clearly placed upon man's own choice. Each man becomes his own Adam.

> Therefore ask no more concerning the multitude of them that perish; for having received liberty they despised the most High, scorned his Law and forsook his ways (8.55-56).

Man in effect should have mastered the evil impulse (imagination) and obeyed the good impulse which was equally open for man to choose to follow. Such a concept of the two impulses is found in the *Testament of Asher:*

> For there are two ways of good and evil, and with these there are two indications in our breast discriminating them. Therefore if the soul takes pleasure in the good (inclination), all its actions are in righteousness; and if it sin it straightway repenteth. For having its thoughts set upon righteousness and casting away wickedness, it straightway overthroweth the evil and uprooteth the sin. But if it incline to the evil inclination, all its actions are in wickedness, and it driveth away the good, and cleaveth to the evil . . . (1.5-8).

All this has the air of over-simplification. It is insufficiently tragic and does not meet the question that still remains. If man sins because of the wrong choice between the two impulses why did God create the evil tendency or impulse in the first place? Even the writer of IV Ezra is not satisfied:

> And I answered and said: 'This is my first and last word; better had it been that the earth had not produced Adam, or else, having once produced him, (for thee) to have restrained him from sinning. For how does it profit us all that in the present we must live in grief and after death look for punishment?
> O thou Adam, what hast thou done?' (IV Ezra 7.116-118).

Here is poignantly expressed the crux between the Law and the Gospel emerging. It is no real help to a man to tell him that he has made the wrong choice between two impulses: If he has what then?

The consequence of believing the possibility of choosing equally freely between two impulses, the good and the evil, are seen in the belief of Judaism in a perfectionist view of man. If man keeps the Law then he is righteous and this is a live option for him. Here the New Testament Gospel takes issue. Especially does Paul bring out the bankruptcy of this view of man's position.

> For I know that nothing good dwells within me, that is, in my flesh. I can will what is right but I cannot do it. For I do not the good I want, but the evil I do not want is what I do (Romans 7.18-19).

Therefore, Paul continues:

> Wretched man that I am! Who will deliver me from this body of death? Thanks be to God through Jesus Christ our Lord! (7.24-25).

Yet it is this insight that is anticipated even in the Old Testament passages in which the word *yetzer* occurs. Not only does the phrase 'every imagination of the thoughts of his heart was only evil continually' (Gen.6.5) occur before the judgment of the flood but also a second time after God had made his covenant with all mankind after the Flood. That is, God makes his Covenant, he renews it not with some reformed mankind but with men whose imaginations are still evil:

> I will never again curse the ground because of man, for the imagination (yetzer) of man's heart is evil from his youth; neither will I ever again destroy every living creature as I have done. While earth remains, seedtime and harvest, cold and heat, summer and winter, day and night, shall not cease (Gen.8.21.22).

Here are majestic words of God's everlasting covenant made with men who are still capable of being subject to an evil bias. It is not of man's deserving but of God's grace that the saving of man comes. There is no easy do-it-yourself method of a man handling his sin. The impulse or bias is there and it is mastered only by a man's acceptance of a greater mastery — that of the Lord Jesus Christ.

# 10. The Prophetic Paradox

'The prophet is a man who feels fiercely. God has thrust a burden upon his soul, and he is bowed and stunned at man's fierce greed. Frightful is the agony of man; no human voice can convey its full terror. Prophecy is the voice that God has lent to the silent agony, a voice to the plundered poor, to the profaned riches of the world. It is a form of living, a crossing point of God and man. God is raging in the prophet's words.' Such is a recent perceptive comment on the Hebrew prophet — the *nabi* — the spokesman. In this we shall seek to answer two questions: What sort of man is the prophet? What are the dominant notes of his message?

*The Prophet and his function*

The function of the prophet may be crystallized in three statements. First, *the prophet is more than one who predicts the future*. In Amos 5.18-19 we have a magnificent short story: "Woe to you who desire the day of the Lord! Why should you have the day of the Lord? It is darkness, and not light; as if a man fled from a lion, and a bear met him; or went into the house and leaned with his hand against the wall and a serpent bit him." The prophet is outlining the consequences of believing in a moral universe. This is not mere prediction of future calamity, but an underlining of God's moral claim in the present situation. The disclosing of the result of wrong action has one aim — to bring people here and now to face the present demands of God. This is more forthtelling than foretelling.

Secondly, *the prophet is more than a social reformer*. It is not accidental that again and again the prophets are seen as figures of great moral stature who protest against every vested interest, economic, political or social. "Is it not for you to know justice? — you who hate the good and love the evil who tear the skin from my people, and their flesh from off their bones; who eat the flesh of my people and flay their skin from them" (Micah 3.2-3). There is the strongest social protest here — and so much more besides! The prophet is more concerned with man's response to God's claim than the assertion of human rights. They must be just because God is just. Finally, *the prophet is One who speaks for Another*. The very word 'prophet' contains the key to the role he plays. It comes from the Greek rendering of the Hebrew root meaning 'to proclaim.' The prophet is one who proclaims his word on behalf of Another — the Other being God. So we have the recurring phrase in the commissioning of the prophets, "the word of the Lord came to me saying" (see Jer. 1.4;2.1; Hosea 1.1; Joel 1.1; Jonah 1.1).

## The Message of Paradox

When we come to examine the word that the prophet speaks on behalf of God, we find a striking paradoxical element. "Almost every prophet brings consolation, promise, and the hope of reconciliation along with censure and castigation. He begins with a *message of doom;* he concludes with a *message of hope."* The God who is Judge is the God who is Redeemer. This double strand is amply illustrated. Hosea can ask: "Shall I ransom them from the power of Sheol? Shall I redeem them from Death?" (Hosea 13.14). The clear answer intended to be understood is No! Yet the same prophet must also affirm in God's name: "I will heal them faithlessness; I will love them freely, for my anger has turned from them. I will be as the dew to Israel; he shall blossom as the lily, he shall strike root as the poplar" (14.4-5). The same paradox is found in younger contemporaries of the same prophet, Micah and Isaiah. Micah, the champion of an oppressed peasantry utters the judgment of God against absentee landlords: "Woe to those who devise wickedness and work evil upon their beds! When the morning dawns, they perform it, because it is in their power of their hand . . . Therefore, thus says the Lord: Behold, against this family I am devising evil, from which you cannot remove your necks; and you shall not walk haughtily, for it will be an evil time" (Micah 2.1-3). Yet the prophet in his closing words is overcome: "Who is a God like thee, pardoning iniquity and passing over transgression for the remnant of his inherit-ance? . . .Thou wilt cast all our sins into the depths of the sea" (Micah 7.18-20). Even in the world of religious cult and ritual the same tension is felt as Isaiah ridicules the externals of a mere religious facade: "What to me is the multitude of your sacrifices? says the Lord; I have had enough of burnt offerings of rams and the fat of fed beasts" (Isa. 1.11-12). The bitterness of the judgment is seen when we realize the scorn behind the names the prophet gives to the leaders of the corrupt society — they have made Zion into another Sodom or Gomorrah (vv. 9-10). Yet the same city shall receive the triumphal procession of the Holy Way, "And the ransomed of the Lord shall return, and come to Zion with singing, with everlasting joy upon their heads; they shall obtain joy and gladness, and sorrow and sighing shall flee away." (35.8, 10).

It is against this background and with this heritage of the prophetic paradox that Christ himself shall claim: "Think not that I come to abolish the law and the prophets; I have come not to abolish them but to fulfil them" (Matt. 5.17). It is in Christ that we see supremely, the One who speaks for Another — Christ, the prophet of God! The Christ who judges and redeems!

# 11. God's Elect

We are all familiar with the great affirmations of Romans 8 in which God himself comes to the side of His people as a judge turned defending counsel:—

"Who shall bring any charge against God's Elect? It is God who justifies; who is to condemn?" God's Elect. This brief study seeks to get behind this characterization of people like ourselves that we may see with greater clarity what God intended when he called us just that.

*The God who Chooses*

This is where we must start. The presupposition of the very existence of the Bible is that God took the initiative and chose His people. We read of this choice in such a passage as Psalm 33:—

Blessed is the nation whose God is the Lord, the people whom He has chosen as His heritage. (v..12). The word bachar — to choose, becomes a technical term to express the fact of election by God. It is used too of God's choice of a King and of his sanctuary. So we read in the account of Saul's coronation:—
And Samuel said to all the people. 'Do you see him whom the Lord has chosen? (1 Samuel 10.24). And further, we have the six-fold refrain in Deuteronomy 12:—
the place which the Lord your God will choose, to make his name to dwell there (v. 11 see also v. 5, 14, 18, 22, 26). The same thought carries on into the description of Jerusalem, the holy city.

For the Lord has chosen Zion; he has desired it for his habitation. This is my resting place for ever; here will I dwell, for I have desired it. (Psalm 132. 13-14).

In all these contexts there is the same theme — it is God who chooses — it is his sovereign choice. The fact of election is central to the Bible record and the consciousness of being chosen, being elected is the very life-blood of the experience behind the record.

### The Choice of the Not Choice

A further characteristic of the use of *bachar* is that it is found in passages that deliberately rule out any idea of God choosing after an intensive examination of the available candidates to be sure he chooses the most worthy or deserving. Two passages illustrate the emphasis upon the mystery of election. God chooses because he chooses. So Moses speaks in God's name immediately after declaring that the Israelites are a people holy to God and his own possession:—

"It is not because you were more in number than any other people that the Lord set his love upon you and chose you, for you were the fewest of all peoples." (Deuteronomy 7.7). And on the very day of crossing the Jordan to possess the Promised Land, Moses must reaffirm that their personal merit does not enter into God's choice:—

"Do not say in your heart, after the Lord your God has thrust them out before you. 'It is because of my righteousness that the Lord has brought me in to possess this land';" (9.4).

The main burden of these passages is well expressed by H. H. Rowley, "Here it is not taught that Israel was chosen because she was better than other nations. Rather was it the miracle of Divine grace that God chose her in her weakness and worthlessness, and lavished His love upon her."

### Chosen to be a Servant

The climax of the Biblical idea of choice or election may be seen in a parallelism that is characteristic of Second Isaiah. The striking feature is found in such passages as:—

"But you, Israel, my servant, Jacob, whom I have chosen, the offspring of Abraham, my friend; you whom I took from the ends of the earth, and called from its farthest corners, saying to you, 'You are my servant, I have chosen you and not cast you off';" (41.8-9).

Again in a passage that is re-echoed in the New Testament (Mt. 12.18-21). "Behold my servant, whom I uphold, my chosen, in whom my soul delights;" (Isaiah 42.1.)

The combination of the ideas of being chosen and of being a servant is found over and over again in Second Isaiah (see 43.10; 44.1-2; 45.4; 49.7). The characteristic of Hebrew parallelism is that the parallel ideas may be used as equivalent terms. In this series of passages the prophet is declaring that, of course, despite the experience of the Exile, the Israelites are the Chosen Nation but that the hall-mark of their election is that they become the Servant Nation. To any who had ideas of being the Top People this must have come as a shock — the essence of being God's Chosen is to be his servant. All the more when we realize that the very people who carried God's people into exile, the heathen nation of Babylon, are among those to be served. Even yet we have not reached the end of the audacity of this interpretation. Not only must the Chosen Elect become Servants as their life role but their service can only be effective through suffering:—

"The Lord God has opened my ear, and I was not rebellious, I turned not backward. I gave my back to the smiters, and my cheeks to those who pulled out the beard; I hid not my face from shame and spitting." (Isaiah 50.5-6).

The voice is that of the Servant who suffers and so proclaims his election.

# 12. The Joy of the Lord

"There is hardly a word so characteristic of the Old Testament as the word joy." Such is the surprising verdict of a major Old Testament scholar. Surprising because one might have expected the word fear or judgment. Yet the evidence is there that Joy is a central Bible motif. In this brief study we shall consider joy as a key to the thought of the Bible. The Hebrew word that is usually translated 'joy' is *simchah*. We shall consider some of the ways in which it is used, together with the New Testament parallel, *chairw* and *chara*.

There are at least four areas of human experience in which Joy is the central theme and enriches our understanding.

## Joy is the expression of Thanksgiving

It is clearly no accident that the initial verdict of God upon his creation is favourable (Gen.1.31) and this is echoed by the psalmist:

> May the glory of the Lord endure for ever, may the Lord rejoice in his works. (Ps.104.31).

The same reaction is found in the response of the sons of God:

> When the morning stars sang together, and all the sons of God shouted for joy. (Job.38.7).

Not only does God rejoice but this attitude of joy is expected to characterize human life as an expression of thankfulness for the continuing gracious acts of God. Men are expected to know joy as an essential part of daily life. So when Moses outlines the choice before the nation of choosing blessing or curse he speaks of the consequences of disobedience in these words:

> Because you did not serve the Lord with joyfulness and gladness of heart, by the reason of the abundance of things . . . therefore you shall serve your enemies. (Deut.28.47-48).

The thought is clear. The people of God ought to be joyful, because they ought to be grateful. Joy is not some subjective feeling of being 'on top of the world,' but the realization of what God had done and being thankful.

*Joy the dominant note of Cult and Law*

A further characteristic of the use of the noun 'joy' *(simchah)* and the verb 'to rejoice' is its integral relation to the ritual of the cult. In describing the ritual associated with the Feast of Tabernacles we read:

> And you shall take on the first day the fruit of goodly trees, branches of palm trees, and boughs of leafy trees, and willows of the brook; and you shall rejoice before the Lord your God seven days. (Lev.23.40).

The divine command to the nation is joyful participation in the cult — have joy!

As with the cultic ritual associated with the festivals, so with the Hebrew law, the Torah. Although it became through the successive narrow interpretations of men, a burden that Jesus himself rejected, this was not the necessary outcome of the Law. At its best, another note is heard in the descriptions of the Law, that of a deep abiding joy. In Psalm 119 we read:

> In the way of thy testimonies I delight as much as in all riches (v.14).

Thy testimonies are my delight, they are my counsellors (v.24).
The opening words of the Psalm that is chosen to open the Psalter make the same link between the demands of the Law and the delight experienced in its service:

> Blessed is the man who walks not in the counsel of the wicked, not stands in the way of sinners, nor sits in the seat of scoffers;

but his delight is in the law of the Lord, and on his law he meditates day and night. (Ps.1.1-2).

## Joy in the life of Jesus

As we turn to the New Testament we are aware that Christ is the Man of Sorrows yet that is not the whole story. His sorrow does not cancel out his joy. The very announcement of the coming of Christ is greeted with joy:

And Mary said, "My soul magnifies the Lord, and my spirit rejoices in God my Saviour, for he has regarded the low estate of his handmaiden.' (Luke 1.46-48).

So, too, the actual birth is an occasion for joy:

Be not afraid; for behold, I bring you good news of a great joy which will come to all the people. (Luke 2.10).

This same note is heard at all the crucial moments of his life. His ministry is described in terms of joy (John 3.29) and the overwhelming emotion after the return of his disciples from their mission is one of joy (Luke 10.17,20).

In the parables of the kingdom, the major motivating force is joy:

The kingdom of heaven is like treasure hidden in a field, which a man found and covered up; then in his joy he goes and sells all that he has and buys that field. (Matt.13.44).

Similarly when Jesus reaches the climax of the parables of the Lost Sheep, the Lost Coin and the Prodigal Son it is hardly accidental that again the dominant mood is one of joy:

Even so, I tell you, there will be more joy over one sinner who repents than over ninety-nine righteous persons who need no repentance (Luke 15.7,10).

It was fitting to make merry and be glad, for this your brother was dead, and is alive; he was lost, and is found. (Luke 15.32).

The end of the journey is no exception. There is joy at his triumphal entry to Jerusalem on Palm Sunday (Matt.21.1-11) and in the Farewell Discourses with his disciples the recurring theme is heard:

These things I have spoken to you, that my joy may be in you, and that your joy may be full (John 15.11, see also 16,20,24; 17.13).

In his birth, his ministry and his death, the note of joy must never be absent if we are to be true to the Bible teaching, yet there is more to be said. His suffering and sorrow cannot be illusory. Here is part of the paradox and mystery illumined by our final affirmation.

### Joy through Suffering

The greatest contribution that the New Testament makes to the Biblical idea of Joy is the repeated conviction that suffering for the sake of Christ is the source of a joy that cannot be gained in any other way. So we have in the Beatitude the word of divine assurance:

> Blessed are you when men revile you and persecute you and utter all kinds of evil against you falsely on my account. Rejoice and be glad, for your reward is great in heaven for so men persecuted the prophets who were before you. (Matt. 5.11-12).

In effect, Jesus offers his congratulations upon the persecution of his disciples and says — now you know what real joy means! In the days of persecution undergone by the Early Church the outcome is the same:

> Without having seen him you love him; though you do not now see him you believe in him and rejoice with unutterable and exalted joy (1 Peter.1.8).

When you come to endure for Christ's sake, says Peter, you won't be able to find words to describe your joy!

Yet another voice pleads that we should be followers of Christ;

> Let us run with perseverance the race that is set before us, looking to Jesus the pioneer and perfecter of our faith, who for the joy that was set before him endured the cross, despising the shame, and is seated at the right hand of the throne of God. (Heb.12.2).

As the Bible commenced with a verdict of favour and joy upon Creation so in the imagery of the New Jerusalem it ends with a promise:

> He will wipe away every tear from their eyes, and death shall be no more, neither shall there be mourning nor crying nor pain any more, for the former things have passed away. (Rev.21.4).

In the pages of the Bible, the story of God's dealings with his people in every generation, there is prohibition and judgment and rightly so. Yet the purpose of the Bible is to bear witness to the abiding joy beyond the suffering and the sorrow. Our privilege is to rejoice and keep on rejoicing!

# 13. The Love that Elects

From the many terms that are used in the Old Testament to express its central affirmation — that God loves his world — there are two major words, *chesed* and *'ahabah*. The first *chesed* represents the loyal love within the covenant relationship and is usually translated 'loving-kindness' in the Authorized Version and 'steadfast love' in the Revised Standard Version. The second word is *'ahabah* and has been translated 'election-love'. It goes further back behind the covenant that God initiated and asks why did God do this? The answer is in this word — because he loved his creation! Because he loved, he elected and because he elected he covenanted.

A brief glance at this term *'ahabah* and the way in which it is used will help us to grasp more certainly the mystery of the love of God.

The word is not a specifically religious one but describes relationships between man and man, man and woman as well as between God and man (See Hos.3.1; Jeremiah 2.2). When used of man and man it expresses the relationship between one who is superior to an inferior and in the rare usage of an inferior attitude to his superior it expresses a love that is both obedient and humble (Deuteronomy 15.16). Our main concern is with God's love for man and the central teaching that stems from this term used to describe God's dealings with men can be summarized in three affirmations that are crystallized in *'ahabah*.

## God's Love is Unconditional

From the human side it is tempting to think that God chose the

Hebrews because of the quality of their national life, their righteousness. The writings of the prophets give little support for this. The only reason they could find for God loving them despite their chronic defecting is that God had made a promise to their fathers long ago: "Yet the Lord set his heart in love upon your farthers and chose their descendants after them, you above all peoples, as at this day" (Deuteronomy 10.15; see also Deuteronomy 9.45).

Yet this is but to push the problem of why God loved his people one stage further back — why did he love their fathers? Nor is there any answer in the suggestion that God saw in the Israelites a religious potential that might under the right conditions blossom forth. The God who was Creator of heaven and earth could have equally well have chosen Moab or the Hittites. On man's side there is no answer. On God's side, he loved them because he loved them. God is like that!

### God's Love involves Creative Action

A second characteristic of 'ahabah — election-love — is its association with the experience of the Exodus. Here the original act of electing the Hebrews to be God's chosen instrument and the event that brought forth the covenant people into being is described as an act of love—the love that elects: "And because he loved your fathers and chose their descendants after them, and brought you out of Egypt with his own presence, by his great power, driving out before you nations greater and mightier than yourselves, to bring you in, to give you their land for an inheritance, as at this day;" (Deuteronomy 4.37; see also Hosea 11.4).

Election-love is far beyond an attitude or frame of mind that is kindly disposed to the object of it. Within the realm of history God expresses his election-love through his intervention in the affairs of the Israelites. For no other reason than that he chose to, he acted. This action of his love created the elect people of God — and all because he wants to save them and so the whole of creation.

### God's Love is a Saving Love

Fundamentally the election-love of God is the expression of God's saving purpose. He creates a covenant relationship because of his love unconditionally and even when the response is not forthcoming from man he will yet work out his purpose. So we have in the prophets this end purpose of God affirmed again and again. "Yet it was I who taught Ephraim to walk, I took them up into my arms; but they did not know that I healed them. I led them with cords of compassion, with the bonds of love, and I became to them as one who eases the yoke on their jaws, and I bent down to them and fed them" (Hosea 11.4). It is the continuing burden of Hebrew prophecy and is the message of the closing contribution: " 'I have loved you,' says the Lord. But you say, 'How hast thou loved us?' " (Mal.1.2) despite a growing and cynical doubt that characterized a spiritually tired people in the aftermath of the return from Exile.

These dominant notes run through the Old Testament. God's sovereign Love is unconditioned by any factor outside his own nature. God's election-love acts in history creating the people who will ultimately respond to his own love. God's love is an expression of his saving purpose.

Yet are not these the self same notes heard with a greater clarity and and force supremely in the person of Christ? It is not altogether surprising that the Greek version of the Old Testament uses *agape* to translate that the Greek version of the Old Testament uses *agape* to translate *ahabah* — election-love and especially in Paul do we find the Hymn to Love that gives the unforgettable picture of what love is in action.

Beyond the detail the dominant pattern emerges clearly:

God's Love is unconditional. He loves us because he loves. (Rom. 11.33).

God's Love enters history supremely in the Incarnation — his loving Word becomes Flesh. (John 1.1-14).

God's Love has one essential purpose — to save the world. (John 3.16).

In our experience we know this to be our story too. In a real and reverent sense, God only knows why He loves us — but he does and we are his church! This love of God is not an attribute of a distant deity but an entering of God into our history — 'as at this day' — the Exodus was always to the Jews a contemporary experience as Calvary is of Today!

This love of God seeks one goal — to bring us back again within his saving purpose — and bring our brother with us!

# 14. God – Our next of kin

The phrase 'next of kin' is usually associated with situations of disaster or sorrow. An appeal is made that they be informed of trouble that has occurred or that they come forward that it can be avoided. 'Next of kin' belongs to a world of crisis. It is just such a world that lies behind the Biblical ideas of redemption and ransom. The essential theme running through the Bible is that God's ultimate purpose is to bring back men into relationship with himself, freeing them from the consequences of alienation. The image of release from captivity or loss of freedom is perfectly appropriate to describe God's saving work as our redeemer!

Behind the theological language are the root ideas that we can briefly examine. The two terms used for taking a man or a thing out of the possession of another by giving an equivalent are *padah* and *ga'al*. So in Exod. 13.13 we have an account of the old edict requiring the giving of the first-born of animal and man to God: "you shall set apart to the Lord all that first opens the womb. All the firstlings of your cattle that are males shall be the Lord's . . . Every first-born of man among your sons you shall redeem" (*padah,* see also Ex. 21.30; Lev. 27.13, 15). The Hebrews clearly compromised by making fixed payments for both infants and animals (Numb. 18.15f). So we have a redeeming or ransoming from death. Other contexts are those of releasing slaves and saving property (Lev. 25.23; Ruth 3.12-13). The two terms are frequently used as parallels (Hos. 13.14; Psalm 69.8) yet they originally had a different emphasis. The word *padah* belongs to the world of ransoming a person or living thing with no reference to the status of the redeemer but the *go'el* is one who belongs to the family circle and assumes the duties and the privileges of the nearest relative. He must stand by his poor relation who may have lost his property or become enslaved. The redeemer is the next of kin (Job. 6.22-23; Ruth 3.12-13). Such is the background of the central affirmation of the Bible that God is our Redeemer. The imagery of ransom and redemption is found especially in Deuteronomy, Second Isaiah and the Psalms (Deut. 7.8; 9.26; 13.5; Isa. 43.1; 44.22-23; 52.9; Ps. 25.22; 26.11; 44.27; 49.15; 103.4). Some of the riches of this interpretation of God's dealing with men can be crystallized in noting the following features of the use of the metaphor.

### Redeeming is an Act of Creation

When Second Isaiah seeks to describe the creation of the world and especially the creation of man, he always stresses the end product of God's purpose, that is, not the creation of man at the beginning but the man who is a saved creation at the end. Creation needs a redeeming before it is complete. So we read, "Awake, awake, put on strength, O arm of the Lord awake as in days of old, the generations of long ago. Was it not thou that didst cut Rahab in pieces that didst pierce the dragon? Was it not thou that didst dry up the sea, the waters of the great deep; that didst make the depths of the sea a way for the redeemed to pass over? And the ransomed of the Lord shall return and come with singing to Zion" (Isa. 51.9-11). The prophet is thinking of God's action in the past at two creative moments: the creation of an ordered world out of a watery chaos and the deliverance from Egypt. The day of deliverance that lies in the future is an act of creation just as much as the first act of creation. So certain is the prophet that his hope is an accomplished fact to him: "But now says the Lord, he who created you, O Jacob, he who formed you, O Israel: 'Fear not, for I have redeemed you (ga'al); I have called you by name, you are mine'" (Isa. 43.1; also 43.7,15; 44.2,21). This is the climax of all redeeming, that man becomes a new creation so that God can say again, You are mine!

To redeem is to re-create.

### Redeeming is an Act of Grace

Between a man redeeming a near relative and God redeeming his people there is a major difference that cannot be over-emphasized. This is the payment of a redemption price, a ransom. The essential point is that God, the Sovereign Lord of all creation, redeems his people through grace — he gives no equivalent when he redeems. He is not involved in a legal process when he expresses his redeeming purpose. Of special significance is the following passage from Second Isaiah: "For I am the Lord your God, the Holy One of Israel, your Saviour. I give Egypt as your ransom. Ethiopia and Seba in exchange for you." (Isa. 43.3 and also Deut. 7.8; Deut. 9.6; Ps. 106.10). Of some thirty-three passages in which God is the one who redeems or ransoms, there is no reference to a ransom price paid by God. In this passage the use of ransom is clearly a rhetorical phrase that underlines the value of his people, his chosen instrument in God's eyes. A number of other passages clearly support this interpretation since they specifically exclude any question of God paying a ransom price. "For thus says the Lord: 'You were sold for nothing, and you shall be redeemed without money'." (Isa. 52.3). And again, " 'I have aroused him in righteousness, and I will make straight all his ways; he shall build my city and set my exiles free, not for price or reward,' says the Lord of hosts." (Isa. 45.13, see also Isa. 55.1). The emphasis upon God's grace as the motive power in his redeeming is all of a piece with the next characteristic of the use of our central terms.


*Redemption is ultimately by God Alone*

This feature may be illustrated from both Old and New Testaments. In Isa. 42.1-4 the Servant is to be the agent of redemption yet as we read further in the fourth Servant Song we have this moving identification of God with his Servant:

"Yet it was the will of the Lord to bruise him; he has put him in grief . . .  he shall see the fruit of the travail of his soul and be satisfied; by his righteous knowledge shall the righteous one, my servant, make many to be accounted righteous; and he shall bear their iniquities" (Isa. 53.10-11). Behind this passage is the self-identification of God with the Servant that is a fore-shadowing of the central New Testament passage: "For the Son of Man came not to be served but to serve, and to give his life as a ransom for many ." (Mark 10.45, see also Matt. 20.28; 1 Tim. 2.6). Here is the new dimension given to redeeming in Biblical thought. God through Christ redeems his people himself. The rigidity of the details of a legal process are out of place in the main stream of Biblical thought — the emphasis is always upon the fact of deliverance and not the method! He alone can free us who have become alienated and he, alone, has done just this.

## Redemption is Present and Future

A final paradox is to be noted. Redemption is both here and now and awaits a future consummation. "In him we have redemption through his blood, the forgiveness of our trespasses, according to the riches of his grace which he lavished upon us." (Ephes. 1.7;, see also Rom. 3.24; 1 Cor. 1.30; Col. 1.14).

Yet also there is the waiting for the final release from all that keeps us alien, apart from God (Ephes. 4.30; Rom. 8.23). God is our Redeemer. He releases us as our next of kin and the four notes of our Bible study are still relevant. Redeeming involves a completing of God's purpose for our lives — a new Creation. Redeeming is of Grace and costs us nothing — but all ourselves. Only God is sufficient for this and he has done this for us — here and now! This is present reality — and there is more to come!

# 3 Concerning Cult and Community

# 15. The Sabbath

"Remember the sabbath day, to keep it holy." This injunction is one of the earliest of the religious sanctions of our lives and represents one of the central parts of the heritage received by the Christian church from Judaism. In this study we shall seek to underline the reasons for the significance of this institution and the present day relevance of its spiritual challenge in modern society.

The word 'sabbath' comes from the Hebrew root *shabath* meaning 'to cease.' So we read in Exodus 23.12: "Six days you shall do your work, but on the seventh day you shall rest; that your ox and your ass may have rest, and the son of your bondmaid, and the alien may be refreshed." The precise origin of the Hebrew Sabbath has sometimes been thought to be associated with the Babylonian sabattu (or sapattu) which is "a day of the quieting of the heart (of the gods)". This day is the day of the full moon at the middle of the month. Certainly in Babylon calendars there are unlucky days such as 7th, 14th, 21st and 28th. These are regarded as evil days and the seventh day quite generally among the ancient Semites was regarded as an evil day which was dominated by evil spirits so that human labour would not prosper and work on this day might antagonize them and so harm the life of the community. It is probable that both the Babylonian and Hebrew days are borrowed from an original Canaanite source.

Although the origins are obscure the significance and usage in Hebrew life is central. With their characteristic ability to borrow from their cultural environment and then transform what they took so the

Hebrews took this rest day of the ancient world and made it the sign of the covenant, a mark that was later to distinguish the Jew from all other peoples.

The central significance of this Hebrew Sabbath can be expressed in a numbers of ways.

### The Sabbath means Resting more than merely Ceasing

Although these ideas are clearly related they are yet distinct. The Hebrew mind wants to set apart a day of the week to be regarded as holy. This means that it belonged to God in the same way that a place was holy, a vessel was holy or a person. "To keep it holy" meant primarily to acknowledge as set apart for his use and so it is sanctified. The emphasis upon the seventh day is not however on one day to the exclusion of the other six but this day takes up into itself all the rest of the week. It consummates all that is done in the other days and offers all back to God in dedication.

The shift from ceasing to resting is significant. It represents the movement from inactivity to activity and the major source is the link with the action of God as described in the Creation account of the priestly writer: "And on the seventh day God finished his work which he had done, and he rested on the seventh day from all his work which he had done. So God blessed the seventh day and hallowed it, because on it God rested from all his work which he had done in creation" (Genesis 2.2-3). Here is a theological advance upon the opening passage referred to in Exodus 23.12 where the dominant reason for the rest on the seventh day is the humanitarian concern for servants and stock.

In this passage the reference is not to a cultic institution but the text speaks, rather, of a rest that existed before man and still exists without man's perceiving it. The declaration mounts, as it were, to the place of God himself and testifies that with the living God there is rest. We must reckon that the emphatic note is that here is a completion and not a negative ceasing. Here is an insight into the nature of God: "The Babylonian creation epic also contains a concluding act following the work of creation; it is the public glorification of the god Marduk, in the assembly of the gods, as the chief gods name his fifty names and extol him. How different, how much more profound, is the impressive rest of Israel's God." (Von Rad, *Genesis*. p.60).

## The Sabbath expresses Joy not Prohibition

The same positive note may be expressed in a further paradox — the Sabbath became for the Israelite a day of joy not of not doing, an abstaining. The negative not working becomes the positive worshipping within a community which experienced the joy of fellowship with God and with each other. So we read immediately after the command to observe the sabbath day: "You shall remember that you were a servant in the land of Egypt, and the Lord your God brought you out thence with a mighty hand and an outstretched arm; therefore the Lord your God commanded you to keep the sabbath day" (Deuteronomy 5.15: see Deuteronomy 16.8-11).

The picture of an interminably long day of doing nothing is completely false as a picture of what the Hebrew meant by the sabbath of the Lord. Now is the time to remember, that is, to make present again the act of God's grace in delivering his people from Egypt and so to rejoice out of sheer gratitude. So with the Sabbath as with the Passover we have the recurring note that God should be worshipped as Sabbath and festival day, "because the Lord your God will bless you in all your prudence and in all the work of your hands, so that you will be altogether joyful" (Deuteronomy 16.15).

> O Sabbath rest by Galilee
> O calm of hills above,
> Where Jesus knelt to share with Thee
> The silence of eternity,
> Interpreted by love.          (Whittier)

## The Sabbath symbolizes Ultimate Victory

A further element in Biblical thinking must be underlined, that is, the forward reference to the future, the time when the people of God will enter into and share the rest of God. Long after the settlement in Canaan one of the psalmists writes: "O that today you would hearken to his voice! Harden not your hearts, as at Meribah, as on the day at Massah in the wilderness, when your fathers tested me, and put me to the proof, though they had seen my work. For forty years I loathed that generation and said, 'They are a people who err in heart, and they do not regard my ways.' Therefore I swore in my anger that they should not enter my rest" (Psalm 95.7-11).

It is this passage that is the stimulus to the author of Hebrews who speaks of the rebellion in the wilderness quoting this psalm. He uses this as the basis of his appeal to his hearers: "Therefore, while the promise of entering his rest remains, let us fear lest any of you be judged to have failed to reach it . . . So then, there remains a sabbath rest for the people of God; for whoever enters God's rest also ceases from his labours as God did from his" (Hebrews 4.1,9).

The affirmation is clear that God's rest is a completion of his purpose, the ultimate victory of all that he intended in the original creation. The rest of Genesis is completed when all his people share too in this victory and know the sabbath rest of God.


### The Sabbath and the Lord's Day

The transition in the Early Church is soon made from the seventh day to the first day of the week because it was the day on which Christ rose from the dead. Now after the sabbath, toward the dawn of the first day of the week, Mary Magdalene and the other Mary went to see the sepulchre. (Matthew 28.1 see also John 20.1, Acts 20.7, 1 Corinthians 16.2). In time we meet the phrase "the Lord's day" (Revelations 1.10) used by the Seer of Patmos.

Although the sabbath and the Lord's Day are distinct, much of the spiritual values are again affirmed in the fuller context. The Lord's Day is more than a ceasing to work, it is a resting of the spirit and a re-creation. It is a day of rejoicing for the greater deliverance from bondage than the Exodus in the Resurrection and the ultimate victory of God is assured through the Risen Lord. He will lead us all into the adventure of God's Sabbath Rest!

# 16. The Power of the Poor

The title is not a revolutionary slogan designed to make an Affluent Society quail or a rallying call for the underprivileged. It is a straight statement of spiritual fact — a fact that Old and New Testaments proclaim again and again.

The words we are concerned with are *ani, anav* that are usually translated "poor, afflicted, humble, meek." Our purpose is to trace the development in the usage of the word in the Old Testament and the impact of its spiritual dimension upon the whole of Biblical thought.

A number of features occur in the usage of "the poor" in the Old Testament.

## *The Poor are God's Special Charge*

We first must note that however much the poor may feel themselves as outcast from human society the Bible affirms repeatedly that they are in the personal protection of God himself: "Sing for joy, O heavens, and exult, O earth; break forth, O mountains, into singing." For the Lord has comforted his people, and will have compassion on his afflicted *ani*,

(Isaiah 49.13). see also the Psalmist's testimony: "Look to him, and be radiant; so your faces shall never be ashamed. This poor man ('ani) cried, and the Lord heard him, and saved him out of all his troubles." (Psalm 34.5-6. see also Psalm 9.12; 10.12.)

It follows naturally that the spokesmen of God will warn against the oppression of the poor of God: Thus says the Lord: "For three transgressions of Israel, and for four, I will not revoke the punishment; because they sell the righteous for silver, and the needy for a pair of shoes — they that trample the head of the poor into the dust of the earth, and turn aside the way of the afflicted." (Amos 2.6-7; see also Ezekiel 22.7; Micah 2.2; 3.5.)

In a number of passages we find special laws concerning the poor and the treatment they must receive: "And when you reap the harvest of your land, you shall not reap your field to its very borders, nor shall you gather the gleanings after your harvest; you shall leave them for the poor and the stranger: I am the Lord your God" (Leviticus 23.22; see Leveticus 19.10; Deuteronomy 15.7-11; 2.14-15.)

## The Poor as the Loyal Remnant

In a number of passages we find the use of *'ani* — the poor — to describe much more than the person who is weak and needy, oppressed by the rich. (Amos 2.7; Isiaih 29.19.) The 'poor' and 'meek' in a number of psalms are thought of as the faithful, God-fearing sons of the Covenant who remain loyal to the prophetic message. They are the representatives of God against his enemies. The significance of the poor transcends social barriers and income brackets. "Why dost thou stand afar off, O Lord? Why dost thou hide thyself in times of trouble? In arrogance the wicked hotly pursue the poor; let them be caught in the schemes which they have devised". (Psalm 10.2) Again we hear the cry: "Remember this, O Lord, how the enemy scoffs, and an impious people reviles thy name. Do not deliver the soul of thy dove to the wild beasts; do not forget the life of thy poor for ever". (Psalm 74.18-19). This last plea to God is occasioned by the destruction of the Temple. We note the relationship between God and his people expressed by *thy* poor. In such passages the 'poor' of God have become the core of resistance to evil and of dedication to the cause of God. (see Psalm 74.22.)

## The Spiritual Challenge of being God's Poor

We are now prepared for a further deepening in the Biblical use of 'poor' that we find in both Old and New Testaments. In the Old Testament there is a striking combining of two characteristics of the ideal Israelite king — his universal power and his humility. The same word *'ani'* is used in the following passage: "Rejoice greatly, O daughter of Zion. Shout aloud, O daughter of Jerusalem. Lo, your King comes to you; triumphant and victorious is he, humble ('ani') and riding on an ass, on a colt the foal of an ass." (Zechariah 9.9). The audacity of this must not be missed. The ruler of the world is the humble one, the poor man of God's choosing. The transition to the New Testament is not difficult. Is not this precisely the spiritual dimension that is expressed in the Beatitudes when Jesus speaking of the nature of his kingship affirms the present reality of Christian happiness and offers his congratulations to those who have become God's Poor: "Blessed are the poor in spirit, for theirs is the Kingdom of heaven". (Matthew 5.3; see also Luke 6.20 which omits 'in spirit.')

What we have now reached is the point where the spiritual challenge of being *'ani* — poor, humble and meek is most clearly expressed. The poor is no longer merely the unfortunate victim of social injustice who keeps protesting against privilege (a reading of the Hebrew prophets will resolve any doubts about whether such protests are made or should be made). Beyond this obvious championing of the poor by God himself is the spiritual insight that a man shows when he sees that every believer before God must act as the poor man who is destitute. He has neither visible nor invisible means of support in himself, but throws himself entirely upon God's mercy.

This is what it means to be poor in Biblical thought and what riches such realization of poverty brings.

# 17. God's Strangers

A frequently occurring term in the Old Testament is — 'stranger' *(ger)*. It is used to describe a person who lives within a community or at a place not inherently his own. So we read of Abraham entertaining the three strangers at Mamre: "He lifted up his eyes and looked, and behold, three men (strangers — *gerim*) stood in front of him. When he saw them, he ran from the tent door to meet them and bowed himself to the earth, and said, 'My lord, if I have found favour in thy sight, do not pass by your servant. Let a little water be brought, and wash your feet, and rest yourselves under the tree, while I fetch a morsel of bread, that you may refresh yourselves, and after that you may pass on since you have come to your servant'." (Gen. 18.2-5). So we read of Abraham going down to Egypt and sojourning there, that is, for a time he would become a *ger* — a stranger or alien. Now there was a famine in the land. So Abraham went down to Egypt to sojourn there, for the famine was severe in the land (Gen. 2.10).

Similarly, Joseph brings his father and his brothers back to be *gerim* — sojourners in the land of Goshen (Gen. 47.1-6) and Jacob describes his stay with Laban as that of being a stranger (ger) (Gen. 32.4).

The *ger* is one who by travelling and settling in a strange place for a longer or shorter period claims protection and sustenance. It comes to mean a special class of citizen who are not born Israelites but who attach themselves to the Israelite community. So we read in the Ten Commandments: "but the seventh day is a sabbath to the Lord your God; in it you shall not do any work, you, or your son, or your daughter, your man-servant or your maid-servant, or your cattle, or the sojourner *(ger)* who is within your gates." (Exod. 20.10).

This Old Testament term *ger* — stranger with the shades of meaning we find in various contexts dominates the interpretation of many later passages, including the New Testament (see Acts 7.6; Ephes. 2.19; Heb. 11.9; 1 Peter 2.11).

We may reach the heart of this Biblical concept as we consider three affirmations that the Bible makes concerning the Stranger *(ger* and in the New Testament *xenos, paroikos)*.

### The Stranger shares in the Covenant

The striking feature of Hebrew law is that there is no suggestion of one law for the native born Hebrew and another for the stranger (ger). Two characteristic notes underline this striking fact. First, the stranger may take part in the Passover festival: "And when a stranger shall sojourn with you and would keep the passover to the Lord, let all his males be circumcised, then he may keep it; he shall be as a native of the land . . . There shall be one law for the native and for the stranger who sojourns among you." (Exod. 12.48-49, see also Lev. 20.2; Ezek 14.7; Numbers 9.14).

Secondly, in the Law of Holiness, we find the words that reach their most profound interpretation and application on the lips of Christ himself: "The stranger who sojourns with you shall be as the native among you, and you shall love him as yourself; for you were strangers in the land of Egypt: I am the Lord your God." This passage is a striking parallel to the verse quoted by Jesus: "but you shall love your neighbour as yourself" (Lev. 19.34 and 19.18, see Matt. 5.43 for the use that Jesus makes in the Sermon on the Mount). It is most moving to find that Jesus himself envisages that the neighbour he commands us to love as ourselves may include the stranger, the alien. In Old and New Testament, it is true to say that the stranger, the outsider shares in the Covenant relationship.

### The Spiritual Dynamic of being a Stranger

A second affirmation is made concerning the *stranger or alien (ger)* in the Old Testament record. We find this underlined in the following tow passages: "You shall not oppress a stranger; you know the heart of a stranger (ger), for you were strangers in the land of Egypt" (Exod. 23.9). It is because God's people have known at first hand the conditions of oppression, of insecurity, of fear and the sense of being isolated from the community that they are commanded never to forget their origins. It is the God who has rescued them from such situations and experiences, who now reminds them that they must act towards others as God has dealt with them. Their first-hand experience will be the very dynamic that will supply the motive for their dealings with all who are strangers and aliens. They have been outside the community and now must never shut others out.

Similarly, we read: "He executes justice for the fatherless and the widow, and loves the stranger *(alien, ger)*, giving him food and clothing. Love the stranger therefore; for you were sojourners in the land of Egypt." (Deut. 10.18-19). If this is the way that God acts towards the alien then let this be your standard as well. In such passages we sense how deeply this experience of being God's strangers has burnt its way into the Hebrew mind and over the centuries it still provides the dynamic for concern and caring.

### The Church of God is the Company of God's Strangers

In both Old and New Testaments we find an extension of the term stranger or alien (NEB) that goes far beyond any social grouping and describes a fundamental spiritual awareness and attitude towards God and man. In the Old Testament we read such passages as: "Hear my prayer, O Lord, and give ear to my cry; hold not thy peace at my tears. For I am thy passing guest, a sojourner (stranger), like all my fathers." (Psalm 39.12).

Again in Psalm 139 we read: "I am a sojourner (stranger, alien) on earth; hide not thy commandments from me." (v.19).

Here the believer in God, one of his chosen people, recognizes that the true relationship between man and God is that of the pilgrim who has no abiding settled abode but as in the days of the desert wanderings of Abraham and later of Moses, he remains one who makes no claim as a settled citizen but one who needs the friendship and hospitality given to a stranger, even an alien.

The same note is found in two New Testament passages, one from the Gospels found in the words of Jesus, and one from the early church records. First, the Gospel scene: "For I was hungry and you gave me food, I was thirsty and you gave me drink, I was a stranger and you welcomer me . . . Truly, I say to you, as you did it to one of the least of these my brethren, you did it to me." (Matt. 25.35;44).

The self-identification of Jesus with the stranger (alien, xenos) can hardly be accidental. Here is the role that this people must play — all are in this spiritual situation. They have no claim to make, only his grace to receive — as a stranger. In this light we may understand the picture described in Hebrews: "These all died in faith, not having received what was promised, but having seen it and greeted it from afar, and, having acknowledged that they were strangers and exiles on the earth. For people who speak thus make it clear that they are seeking a homeland . . . Therefore God is not shamed to be called their God, for he has prepared for them a city." (Heb. 11.13-16).

This is the authentic spiritual attitude of God's people, the continuing church — they are strangers, aliens for whom a homeland, and an abiding city is prepared, where they may rejoice that God's strangers may return home.

# 18. The Way of the Lord

"The primary image to express conduct or behaviour in the Old Testament is the 'way' or 'road' (*derek*)." A recent work of Old Testament research has selected this theme as a motif that is so rich and manifold in its usage that it can be used to express the heart of the relationship between man and man and God and Man. (See J. Muilenberg, *The Way of Israel*). In this short study our purpose is to sketch some of the ways, colour and emphases which the idea of the way brings to the Bible story.

The word quoted in the opening sentence, *derek* (way, road) comes from the verb *darak* which has a basic meaning of 'to tread, trample down.' In the use made of this root we find the original physical action of treading in the line from the Song of Deborah, "March on, my soul, with might!" (Judges 5.21). Here the treading has become marching. The action of actual trampling is seen in Amos 9.13 with its picture of a time of renewal and abundance. "Behold, the days are coming," says the Lord, "when the plowman shall overtake the reaper and the treader of grapes him who sows the seed." The verbal form translated 'treader' has the same root as the command to march had in the previous passage. A further illustration of the use of darak is found in Isaiah 5.28 where we read, "their arrows are sharp, all their bows bent, their horses' hoofs seem like flint, and their wheels like the whirlwind." The reference is to Assyrian forces who will be used by God to punish the Israelites for their rebellion against God. The phrase 'bows bent' is literally 'bows trodden down,' that is ready for action with the foot already bending the bow.

From these introductory comments we can see that there is a sense of activity and energy connected with the original idea and this we can examine further as we outline the main ideas associated with The Way *(derek)*.

## Way as representing a Character of Life

In a number of passages we find that from the physical sense of treading a road or path that leads from one place to another, *derek* is used for a quality of behaviour, a character of living relationships.

This usage is found in the writings of prophet and psalmist and echoed again by the wisdom writers. In Jeremiah 6.27 he speaks of his mission as one who must test precious metals for the spurious dross and records the commission of God to him: "I have made you an assayer and tester among my people, that you may know and assay their ways" (see also 7.23 where God refers again to the way that he commands). The psalmists again and again underline this theme of the Way of life when he pleads: "Make me to know thy ways, O Lord; teach me thy paths." He continues to describe the guidance that God gives: "He leads the humble in what is right, and teaches the humble his way." "Lead me in thy truth, and teach me, for thou art the God of my salvation; for thee I wait all the day long." (Psalm 25. 4,9,5).

The parallelism between way and truth and what is right clearly indicates that *derek* is now used for the character of personal behaviour. What is more here is not a way that is discovered by human ingenuity but a way, a quality of living, that presupposes the guidance and leadership that God alone can give.

This is amply illustrated by the wisdom writers in Proverbs. So we read of the invitation of personified Wisdom and the beatitude she offers: "And now, my sons, listen to me: happy are those who keep my ways. Hear instruction and be wise, and do not neglect it. Happy is the man who listens to me, watching daily at my gates, waiting beside my doors." (Proverbs 8.32-34).

## The Challenge of the Two Ways

Because the way of a man came to stand for the character of his behaviour and conduct it follows that if there is to be any truth, any spiritual reality, there must be a free choosing of the way in which a man should go. This doctrine of the two ways becomes clearly articulated throughout scripture, in both Old and New Testaments. Some notable examples are to be found in the following passages. In the farewell discourse of Moses to the assembled nation we read: "See, I have set before you this day life and death, good and evil. If you obey the commandments of the Lord your God which I command you this day, by loving the Lord your God, by walking in his ways, and keeping his commandments..." (Deuteronomy 30.15-16). The whole future of the nation is to hinge on this choice of the Lord's way. As in the Hebrew law, so with the nation's songs. In Psalm 1 which serves as a crystallization of the whole Psalter the issues before the nation are once again clearly articulated and summed up in the verdict of the closing verse: "For the Lord knows the way of the righteous, but the way of the wicked will perish" (v.6). In Hebrew thought the word 'knows' has the undertone of fellowship and intimacy. Here it carries the sense of God's approval and acceptance. The way of the wicked man, of course, God knows about, that is, he is not ignorant of it, but at the same time he rejects it. Throughout the Bible record the choice is sharpened as the figure of Wisdom again offers her choice. Should a man not seek wisdom when "Her ways are ways of pleasantness, and all her paths are peace"? (Prov.3.17). Yet Wisdom also warns, "For he who finds me finds life and obtains favour from the Lord; but he who misses me injures himself; all who hate me love death" (Prov.8.35-36). In the New Testament the same doctrine of the two ways appears in the passage from Matthew: "Enter by the narrow gate; for the gate is wide and the way is easy, that leads to destruction, and those who enter by it are many. For the gate is narrow and the way is hard, that leads to life, and those that find it are few" (Matthew 7.13-14). (Here *hodos* is the parallel to Hebrew *derek*).

### The Community of the Way

In the New Testament we find a number of passages in which "way" is used without any other qualification or description and in these contexts clearly refers to a fellowship and community of those who belong to the Way. So we have in Acts the well-known description of Saul's objective: "But Saul, still breathing threats and murder against the disciples of the Lord, went to the high priest and asked him for letters to the synagogues at Damascus, so that if he found any belonging to the Way, men or women, he might bring them bound to Jerusalem"

(Acts 9.2). From opponent he turns to advocate and at Ephesus we read, "he entered the synagogue and for three months spoke boldly, arguing and pleading about the Kingdom of God; but when some were stubborn and disbelieved, speaking evil of the Way before the congregation, he withdrew from them, taking the disciples with him, and argued daily in the hall of Tyrannus" (Acts 19.8-9. See also v.23; and 22.4). In Paul's reply to Tertullus before Felix he affirms: "But this I admit to you, that according to the Way, which they call a sect, I worship the God of our fathers, believing everything laid down by the law or written in the prophets, having a hope in God which these themselves accept, that there will be a resurrection of both the just and the unjust" (Acts 24.14-15). The underlying sense of community, a belonging together rather than an individual's private acceptance of a way of living, is here a working out of the relationship of being the Covenant people. The Community of the Way in the New Testament is the precise parallel to Covenant People of the Old Testament. "Obey my voice, and I will be your God, and you shall be my people; and walk in all the way that I command you that it may be well with you" (Jeremiah 7.23; also for this theme Deuteronomy 5.32; Exodus 18.20).

*Christ the Way*

The climax of Biblical thought concerning the Way is the affirmation made by Christ himself in answer to the mystified Thomas as Jesus seeks to prepare his disciples for his departure: "Jesus said to him, 'I am the way, and the truth, and the life; no-one comes to the Father, but by me'." (John 14.6).

Here there is no question of way meaning a certain standard of behaviour. Christ through his life and Resurrection embodies all that the Bible has said about the Way. In him there is to be found the dynamic that creates a character of living. In him men's choices are

brought to a head —to crucify or to crown?

It is no wonder that the difference that Christ has made was so movingly described centuries ago: "Therefore, brethren, since we have confidence to enter the sanctuary by the blood of Jesus, by the new and living way . . . ." (Hebrews 10.20).

This is the way that he has brought us, to himself the new and living Way. So we must

Run the straight race through God's good grace,

Lift up thine eyes and seek His face;
Life with its way before us lies;
Christ is the path, and Christ the prize.

# 19. The Ark of the Covenant – Furniture or Faith?

In the early history of the Hebrews the focal point of the sanctuary is the Ark of the Covenant. According to a late description the Ark was a rectangular chest with poles for transporting, with two winged cherubim and a lid called the mercy seat with a protective curtain and inside the two tables of the law (see Exodus 25.10-22; Hebrews 9.3.).

Yet the detailed description of an article of ecclesiastical furniture does scant justice to what through Old and New Testaments is essentially an instrument of living, dynamic faith.

From the contexts in which reference to the Ark of the Lord is made (other titles are Ark of the Covenant or Ark of Testimony) four main features emerge and are worthy of comment.

*The Ark represents the Power of God*

We find this emphasis on dynamic power in such passages as Joshua 3 and 1 Samuel 5. In the first context the scene is that of Joshua leading the Israelites across Jordan: "And when the soles of the feet of the priests who bear the ark of the Lord, the Lord of all the earth, shall rest in the waters of the Jordan, the waters of Jordan shall be stopped from flowing, and the waters coming down from above shall stand in one heap." (Joshua 3.13). Again in Ashdod after the Philistines had captured the ark of God and set it up in the Temple of Dagon the following morning worshippers are met with this scene: "And when the people of Ashdod rose early next day, behold, Dagon had fallen face downward on the ground before the ark of the Lord." (1 Samuel 5.3).

This does not mean that Dagon was insecurely propped up but that Dagon the god was making obeisance to God. Such is the power associated with the Ark of God that Jordan is crossed and heathen gods submit.

## The Ark symbolizes the Presence of God

Long before the Ark was placed in the place of honour in the Temple, it stood for the guiding God who led his people through the wilderness. Kept in a tent because there is the restless vitality of God on the Move who will not be tied down to a particular place. So Nathan speaks to David at God's command. "Thus says the Lord: 'Would you build me a house to dwell in? I have not dwelt in a house since the day I brought up the people of Israel from Egypt to this day, but I have been moving about in a tent for my dwelling'." (2 Samuel 7.5-6). The Ark embodies the nation's history, a nomad's shrine that never ceases to speak of God's saving prsnce with their fathrs and with every generation. "And let them make me a sanctuary, that I may dwell in their midst." (Exodus 25.8). It is through the Ark at this time that God becomes Immanuel — God with us.

## The Ark is an Extension of God Himself

The evidence concerning the Ark goes even further. In a number of passages the Ark is referred to as God in Person, that is, an extension of his personality. Especially do we find this in Numbers 10.35: "and whenever the ark set out, Moses said, 'Arise, O Lord, and let thy enemies be scattered; and let them that hate thee flee before thee.' And when it rested, he said, 'Return, O Lord, to the ten thousand thousands of Israel'." (See also 1 Samuel 6.3,5,8,20). In such passages there is no distinction in the thought of the time between the ark and the Lord. Throughout the Eastern world the symbol and the reality symbolized are seen as a unity. Here we see a pointer to the secret of every religious symbol and not least the Cross and the Table of the Lord in the Christian Church (see Mark 14.22-25; 1 Corinthians 11.23-26). The Ark in Hebrew thought was an extension of God, as much as his word and his spirit. Not only his throne (Jeremiah 3.16) and footstool (Ezekiel 43.7) but God himself (Psalm 132.8).

## The Ark and the People of God

A final truth emerges from the Biblical evidence concerning the Ark — that the Church itself becomes the living reality for today precisely parallel to the Ark in ancient Israel. A number of passages support this line of thought. The probable latest appearance would be in the reign of Josiah (Jeremiah 3.16). The very teaching of Jeremiah envisages a situation when he hopes that in the new, the re-born Israel, the Law of God will no longer be taught by one man to another, because it is written in people's hearts. (Jeremiah 31.31ff.). Then there will be no need any longer for an Ark where the *autographon* (the original divine manuscript) of the Law is kept. This insight is developed in the fact that in the Second Temple the Holy Place is empty — no ark because the whole Temple is the House of God (see Ezekiel 48.35 for the name of the holy city — the Lord is there). We are thus prepared for the New Testament passages in which Jesus says: "Destroy this temple, and in three days I will raise it up. The Jews then said, 'It has taken forty-six years to build this temple, and will you raise it up in three days?' But he spoke of the temple of his body." (John 2.19-21). See also Colossians 1.19f; 2.9). In Ephesians 2.20-22 Paul takes up the theme of the living Temple when he speaks of the new life in Christ and the household of God as "built upon the foundation of the apostles and prophets, Christ Jesus himself being the chief corner-stone, in whom the whole structure is joined together and grows into a holy temple in the Lord; in whom you also are built into it for a dwelling place of God in the Spirit."

As we bring these strands together we realise afresh that there is a real issue behind the Biblical references to the Ark of the Covenant—it can be a matter of Furniture or of Faith.

The challenge to the Christian individual and corporate is:

Dare we complete the Bible expectation and hope:

in expressing the power of God?
in embodying the presence of God?
in being as the Divine Ark for the New Israel in the modern wilderness of uncommitted people, groping people — the covenant of God himself to this world?

# 20. Remember Tomorrow!

Throughout the Bible there is a continuing call of God to his people — found in both positive and negative form — Remember — Forget not! At first sight, this might seem an admission that the Bible is concerned with wistfully looking back over our shoulders and longing for the good old days! Any such idea is soon exploded when we consder the way in which the word usually translated 'to remember,' *zakar,* is used. The essential note behind this Old Testament word in not so much a recalling of a past that is gone but a re-creating of the past, a bringing into the present a reality that the past cannot confine nor contain. The act of remembering is an act of audacity, of affirmation.

In four Bible scenes we may feel the challenge of God's call to remember and forget not!

*Remembrance re-enacts an act of Deliverance*

The great experience that God's people are urged again and again to remember is that of the Exodus from Egypt. So we read:

> Remember this day, in which you came out from Egypt, out of the house of bondage, for by strength of hand the Lord brought you from this place (Exod. 13.3).

This is the experience that has burnt its way into the very imagination of the people of God. They must never forget that above all they are delivered people — this the very act that brought them into existence they must remember. It is in such an act of remembering that each generation must re-create for itself the relationship betwen God and man anew.

The same note is heard in the pleading of Moses in God's name that the people of God prepare themselves to enter the Promised Land and possess it:

> And you shall remember all the way which the Lord God has led you these forty years in the wilderness, that he might humble you, testing you to know what was in your heart, whether you would keep his commandments, or not (Deut. 8.2; see also vv. 11-14).

The only spiritual security the people of God had known in the desert had been that the same God who had delivered them from Egypt was now leading them through their wilderness trials — this crucial experience they were never to forget in the new world of promise that lay in front of them. To remember the past was to undergird the present.

### Remembrance that is a Denial of God

The scene now changes from the exodus and wilderness to another major moment in the experience of God's people — that of Exile. At a time when the hopes of the nation were low and a fatalism had infected the thinking of the nation, in a strange land they were desolate. God speaks through an unknown voice of the Second Isaiah:

> Remember not the former things
> nor consider the things of old.
> Behold, I am doing a new thing;
> now it springs forth do you not perceive it?
> I will make a way in the wilderness
> and rivers in the desert. (Isaiah 43.18-19).
> Saying to the prisoners, 'Come forth,' to those who are in
> darkness, 'Appear.'
> They shall feed along the ways,
> on all bare heights shall be their pasture;
> they shall not hunger or thirst,
> Neither scorching wind nor sun shall smite them,

for he who has pity on them will lead them,
and by springs of water will guide them.
And I will make all my mountains a way,
and my highways shall be raised up. (Isaiah 49.9-11).

At first sight, this seems a contradiction of the main theme of this study — Remember not! Yet a glance at the whole passage gives the clue. The danger they are in is that they wistfully remember the good old days when they were in their homeland, when they could share in the worship of the Temple. Now with their Temple in ruins, and in this alien setting what could they do? The prophet has no doubt. They must not look back and remember what God has done as if he could not do it again! This is the new thing he is doing, and this the new song they must sing — that God is going to bring them through another and even greater Exodus out of the dread Exile situation. Do not, says the prophet, remember it as if that is all over and done with but realise that what you remember as happening to your fathers is now — before your very eyes — happening to you! The reality of remembering involves a present certainty and we must ever remember what God has done in a way that does not deny his continuing power and concern.

*Remembering as a Sacrament*

From the wilderness and exile the scene changes to the Upper Room and the Lord's Supper, as Paul describes the setting:

> For I received from the Lord what I also delivered to you, that the Lord Jesus on the night when he was betrayed took bread, and when he had given thanks, he broke it, and said, 'This is my body which is for you. Do this in remembrance of me.' In the same manner also the cup, after supper saying, 'This is the new covenant in my blood. Do this, as often as you drink it, in remembrance of me.' (1 Cor. 11.23-25).

The whole gospel would be bankrupt if what Jesus meant was that after his death he would be glad to be remembered rather than forgotten! Jesus and Paul, both Jews, would know full well that the look back to the Passover Meal which must have been in their minds, would only reaffirm the great victory of the Exodus that brought God's people into being. What God had done at the Exodus and after the Exile, he would now do for the Early and continuing Church. Here is a renewal of the Covenant Relationship —a remembering that guarantees the victory of God's purpose today and tomorrow! This is far more than a nostalgic sighing after yesterday. It is this certainty about the future outcome that dominates our thinking about the Sacrament — as we remember and in that remembering commit ourselves anew.

### Remembrance through the Spirit

A final scene from the New Testament speaks of the promise of Jesus to his followers as he prepares their mind and hearts for his departure:

> But the Counsellor, the Holy Spirit, whom the Father will send in my name, he will teach you all things, and bring to your remembrance all that I have said to you. (John 14.26).

It is supremely through His Spirit that we are reminded of Christ's promises concerning the future as well as the past. This is a remembering that belongs to Tomorrow. Every generation is reminded by the Spirit of what God has done, is doing and will yet do. There is a Present and Future Reality about the Risen Lord. He is Present again and will be in my Tomorrow. The Road to Tomorrow leads through Yesterday as we Remember the One who is Present Again!

# 21. The Year of the Trumpet

In a number of Biblical passages we find reference to a time of rejoicing that is called a time of Jubilee. It is clearly an occasion of joy:

> And you shall hallow the fiftieth year, and proclaim liberty throughout the land to all its inhabitants; it shall be a jubilee for you, when each of you shall return to his property and each of you shall return to his family. (Lev. 25.10).

We find the same note used by Jesus himself as a he issues his manifesto for his ministry when he returns to the synagogue in Nazareth, his home town, and reads from the prophet Isaiah:

> because he has anointed me to preach good news to the poor
> and recovering of sight to the blind,
> He has sent me to proclaim release to the captives
> And recovering of sight to the blind,
> and set at liberty those who are oppressed,
> to proclaim the acceptable year of the Lord (Luke 4.18-19).

Jesus expresses his deepest purpose in these words that end with referring to the ancient Hebrew institution of Jubilee which lies behind the words 'the acceptable year of the Lord.'

What are the central ideas behind this usage? The word 'Jubilee' itself comes from the original Hebrew word *yobel* which is used of the ram's horn which is blown only by the priests and has a greater sanctity and supernatural effect than the ordinary trumpet (the shophar). It is called the great trumpet since it is the blast from this that ushers in the fiftieth year with all that it implied for the Hebrew people. It is the year of Jubilee, that is indeed the Year of the Trumpet (See Isa. 27.13; Lev. 23.24).

Behind this term, Jubilee, four affirmations may be discerned

## The Year of Jubilee means Release from Burdens

An overall note of rejoicing at being released from burdens is the first dominant note in the idea of Jubilee.

> And if your brother becomes poor beside you, and sells himself to you, you shall not make him serve as a slave; he shall be with you as a hired servant and as a sojourner. He shall serve with you until the year of Jubilee; when he shall go out from you, he and his children with him, and go back to his own family, and return to the possession of his fathers. For they are my servants, whom I brought out of the land of Egypt; they shall not be sold as slaves. (Lev. 25.39-42).

It is highly significant that the motivation is once again as so often in the Old Testament, the experience of being brought out of bondage, in Egypt. Because they have all been aware of what it means to bear the burden of oppression and to know the release that God brought to his own people through the Exodus so they must release all of their fellows from their burdens in the year of Jubilee. As the year of release would draw near, one could sense the expectancy of the burdens being removed. This should be reminder enough to owner and servant, employer and employee of the very beginning of being God's Chosen People. The dynamic is one of spiritual insight not a piece of enlightened social engineering.

## Jubilee means a Return to the Homeland

The second feature of the celebration of Jubilee is that the exile and stranger, the sojourner, would now have the chance to return to his homeland, to his own kith and kin, the land of his fathers!

> And it shall be a jubilee for you, when each of you shall return to his property and each of you shall return to his family (Lev. 25.10).

The return home means that there is a positive side to the occasion of Jubilee. Not only a release from burdens but the chance to pick up again the threads of home and family life with a man's own community. He can once more realise the spiritual freedom that comes from a sense of belonging. In the Hebrew mind there is not possible any idea of a man in isolation, an individual. A man becomes a real person only in community and nowhere more than in his own community. It is this restoration to the community that could nourish him, that the year of Jubilee brings. Back in this spiritual and physical homeland, "the possession of his fathers" he could become a full man again.

### Jubilee means a Renewal of God's Claim

A third emphasis behind the celebration of Jubilee is that through this institution God is seen to renew his claim upon the nation's land and the nation's life.

> The land shall not be sold in perpetuity, for the land is mine; for you are strangers and sojourners with me. (Lev. 25.23).

Here is an affirmation of the Lordship of God. God alone can be the real possessor of the land since he created it in the first place. So, too, no man can own either another man or his land because it is God alone who should make a total claim upon another human being. It is God who has given and he alone can take away (See Gen. 1.28; 2.15; Job 1.21). Because neither a man nor his land can be owned for ever by another, the year of Jubilee crystallizes this claim of God upon his world. It is his world and only in response to his renewed claim can we manage either our possessions or our personal relationships.

### Jubilee depends upon the initiative of God

We have seen briefly something of the spiritual dynamic behind the Hebrew year of Jubilee. The dominant motive is always related to the act of God when he delivered his people from oppression through the Exodus. This dread burden must never again be laid upon any member of this people, and as they see their world role, nor upon any other creature of God, since he is Lord of all. This source of spiritual power is much profounder than a concern for each other's welfare. It is the deeper claim of God that one people, even his chosen people, can never be good enough to own or control the lives of others.

So today in God's name, his people, his church must hear again the notes of the trumpet — the jubilee — as we proclaim the day of release.

Our burdens he alone can lighten. We return to our spiritual homeland, the fellowship of the Church and reaffirm that we acknowledge his renewed claim upon our lives. This is the same manifesto that our Lord made at Nazareth and he demands that we make it a reality for our time.

# Reading List

J. J. von Allmen (ed.) *Vocabulary of the Bible,* Lutterworth, 1956.

B. W. Anderson, *The Living World of the Old Testament,* Longman, Green, 1958.

E. Jacob, *Theology of the Old Testament,* Hodder and Stoughton, 1958.

E. Jones, *The Greatest Old Testament Words,* SCM, 1964.

E. Jones, *The Living Word,* REP, 1968.

L. Koehler, *Old Testament Theology,* Lutterworth, 1957.

A. Richardson (ed.), *A Theological Word Book of the Bible* SCM, 1950.

W. Gordon Robinson, *Living Words and their Meanings,* Denholm House Press, 1968.

H. H. Rowley, *The Faith of Israel,* SCM, 1956.

N. H. Snaith, *The Distinctive Ideas of the Old Testament* Epworth, 1944.

T. C. Vriezen, *An Outline of Old Testament Theology,* Blackwell, 1958.


## MORE ADVANCED WORKS

James Barr, *The Semantics of Biblical Language,* OUP, 1961.

W. Eichrodt, *Theology of the Old Testament,* SCM, vols. I and II, 1961 and 1967.

G. von Rad, *Old Testament Theology,* vols. I and II, Oliver and Boyd, 1962 and 1965.